Freedom of Information

Freedom of Information

Working towards compliance

LIZ TAYLOR

Chandos Publishing

Oxford · England · New Hampshire · USA

Chandos Publishing (Oxford) Limited
Chandos House
5 & 6 Steadys Lane
Stanton Harcourt
Oxford OX29 5RL
UK
Tel: +44 (0) 1865 884447 Fax: +44 (0) 1865 884448
Email: info@chandospublishing.com
www.chandospublishing.com

Chandos Publishing USA
3 Front Street, Suite 331
PO Box 338
Rollinsford, NH 03869
USA
Tel: 603 749 9171 Fax: 603 749 6155
Email: BizBks@aol.com

First published in Great Britain in 2004

ISBN:
1 84334 103 4 (paperback)

© L. Taylor, 2004

British Library Cataloguing-in-Publication Data.
A catalogue record for this book is available from the British Library.

Cover images courtesy of Bytec Solutions Ltd (*www.bytecweb.com*) and David Hibberd (*DAHibberd@aol.com*).

Printed in the UK by 4Edge Limited - www.4edge.co.uk

Contents

Acknowledgements

There are a great number of people who have all had a part to play in shaping my thoughts as to how FOI could be dealt with. Most important to mention are all the colleagues I have worked with over the past nine months. Through their contributions of business knowledge to FOI preparations, they have enabled me to identify a large number of FOI related issues, many of which I have developed in this book.

URLs

At the time of publication, all website addresses contained in this book were correct.

At the time of going to print the Section 60 Code of Practice under FOISA was still in draft and had yet to be laid before the Scottish Parliament.

About the author

Liz Taylor has worked towards preparing for Freedom of Information (FOI) in a number of public sector organisations across the UK for the past three years. Currently the FOI project manager at the Highlands and Islands Enterprise, Liz previously worked for the Qualifications and Curriculum Authority where she initiated the records management project.

Prior to this, Liz was a training manager in the Royal Navy for six years, during which time she managed projects to ensure personnel systems were compliant with the Data Protection Act 1998.

With a background in knowledge and information management, Liz has expertise in developing effective business processes, which has enabled the successful delivery of many practical initiatives, particularly when dealing with legislation.

Liz and her husband also manage their own tourist and hospitality business in the North-west Highlands of Scotland.

The author be contacted at:

liz@housebytheloch.co.uk.

Introduction to Freedom of Information legislation

Background

As from 1 January 2005, Freedom of Information (FOI) legislation comes fully into force across the United Kingdom (UK). In the long term, FOI has the potential to have a profound effect on the way in which the public sector manages information, leading to more open and transparent way of working. However, in the short term it is essential organisations take the necessary measures to achieve compliance and are ready for the introduction of FOI. Sound and considered preparations will help minimise detrimental effects on existing business processes, resulting from inadequate resourcing and insufficient planning. Devising a suitable programme of activities to meet the requirements of FOI will also enable your organisation to manage any associated risks.

This short book is designed to aid some of the practical preparations required for FOI, offering an interpretation of some of the implications for your organisation. The main focus is upon being able to process requests for information once FOI comes into force although some aspects will also contribute to other compliance issues. It is important to note that reading this book will not achieve compliance for your organisation. It is intended to help you identify where non-compliance could occur, and assist you in recognising the factors that should be included in activities to address those issues in your particular organisation.

The book complements guidance and advice already available about other elements of complying with FOI such as records management (RM) and the management of publication schemes. It, therefore, does not cover RM or the development of schemes in any detail, as there is already a vast amount of useful literature and guidance published. This information is available from a variety of websites and publications, some of which are referenced throughout.

There are two Acts that are of importance in the context of this book: Freedom of Information Act 2000 (FOIA) which applies to the UK with the exception of Scotland and Freedom of Information (Scotland) Act 2002 (FOISA) which will come into force throughout Scotland. There is a substantial amount of similarity between the two Acts (and they are referred to jointly as 'FOI' or 'the Acts' throughout the book), although the differences are highlighted where necessary. Both Acts refer to codes of practice, which also place obligations on organisations (although non-statutory) and, therefore, should be taken into consideration when planning any programme of preparation. Again, these are referenced throughout the book where relevant.

Records and information management has, in many public sector organisations, lacked the dedicated skills and resources over recent years. FOI provides an ideal opportunity to re-evaluate the importance of information and the role it plays in delivering organisational objectives. The need to accurately assess information management (IM) requirements from a business perspective in conjunction with those of FOI is vital to ensure information is not managed purely to comply with FOI. This approach has the potential to adversely affect business efficiency. Improvements to information flows and overall effectiveness may offer benefits to your organisation and be a positive outcome of preparations and are therefore emphasised throughout the text.

Basic facts about the Acts

The list of organisations that fall within the scope of FOI is extensive. For confirmation about your own organisation you should check the relevant Act and also consult with the appropriate commissioner if you are unclear about your obligations. You also need to be certain about which Act you fall under; for example, UK-wide public authorities will fall under FOIA, regardless of whether or not they have offices in Scotland.

Both Acts provide a general right of access or entitlement to information held by public authorities and place two core requirements on public authorities:

- to produce and maintain a publication scheme, a document that details the classes of information that an organisation will routinely make available;
- to process requests for information held by that authority.

On an applicant submitting a request for information, authorities have 20 working days in which to respond to that request. An authority has to fulfil a number of obligations:

- in the majority of cases, to confirm whether or not the information is held (for further details see Chapter 5 as the two Acts are slightly different in this area. This is not a specific duty under FOISA);

- to provide the information if it is held by the authority unless it is subject to an exemption.

Requests do not have to mention FOI and can be made to anyone within a public sector organisation. Timing towards the 20 working-day obligation generally begins on receipt of the request and consequently it is vital that everyone in the organisation understands that any request for information from any applicant falls under FOI.

There is no requirement for an applicant to state why they have requested the information or for what purpose they intend to use it, although copyright legislation may apply to some information held by your organisation. There are also a number of factors that cannot be taken into account when deciding whether or not to release information, which include any subsequent embarrassment that may be suffered by the organisation. These factors are further discussed in Chapter 5.

The key principles of the legislation are described above, but before beginning to assess the practical implications of FOI it is important that you have a general understanding of the legislation. This book is not intended to be a legal interpretation and, therefore, you need to identify any issues your organisation may have, which this book should help you to do, and take advice where appropriate. Additionally, while specifics of the Acts are further discussed where relevant in the following chapters, the book will not necessarily give you the full overview required by your particular organisation. There are already a number of sources that provide good summaries of FOI which will provide you with alternative discussions about the Acts. Some of these are referenced throughout this book.

Preparation for FOI is absolutely essential to ensure that your organisation benefits from changes in the way in which it manages information and is able to manage any new risks which FOI presents. A lack of preparation is likely to result in an uncontrolled and mismanaged response to FOI. Crisis management will inevitably present a number of problematic issues to your organisation, which may include non-compliance and damage to organisational reputation. Lack of management is also likely to have significant resource implications once the FOI comes into force, which could have detrimental affects on core business processes that will be very difficult to quantify and control.

How to use this book

Each chapter has been written to address a specific topic, enabling the reader to selectively choose, first, what they read and, second, in which order they deal with compliance issues. The book has been designed in this way, as organisational priorities are likely to dictate the order and priority in which compliance initiatives are dealt with, and therefore may be different across a range of organisations.

Each chapter starts by setting objectives and then has a short, descriptive section about the topic which explains why action is necessary and puts initiatives into the context of FOI. The main part of each of the chapters are the checklists that will initially enable you to gauge which initiatives are likely to be required within your organisation, and then monitor how much progress has been made.

The checklists are written as questions and you may ask why there are so many questions with very few answers. This book has been written to help organisations consider the factors involved in preparing for FOI. It is likely that no two organisations will be dealing with the same set of issues to ensure compliance, although the way in which they respond to issues will be influenced by similar factors. Organisations may also prioritise the issues that they have to deal with differently. Consequently, the questions should enable most organisations to consider the majority of factors associated with each topic.

It is important to note that there are no right or wrong answers to the majority of questions on the checklists, as the response will in many instances depend on your organisation. Furthermore, there may be some questions that are not relevant to your organisation or issues you have already identified that are not covered by the book. The checklist is not intended to be an exhaustive list but a guide to shaping preparations, which need to be developed and taken forward for your organisation to achieve compliance. Each of the questions raised about requirements for FOI is followed by some advice and guidance on how to accurately assess and, if deemed necessary, meet each of the criteria.

At the end of each chapter there is a summary of points that the checklists should have helped you address followed by a section of useful references, which lists literature that may help with the tasks in hand.

Topics

This book covers a range of topics, all of which specifically deal with the practical issues surrounding FOI implementation. The first two topics look at how to begin preparations and what you should establish about the current status of your organisation prior to identifying new activities associated with FOI. The key part of the book is at Chapter 4, which examines the procedures that need to be in place in order to make information accessible. One issue of these procedures is examined separately in the following chapter, which looks at the principles of managing exemptions. The final three chapters provide a very brief introduction to other areas that may be associated with making information available and dealing with audit trails, training and evaluating the success of your preparations. Each of the topics are summarised briefly in the sub-sections below.

Where to start

Before starting with any initiative or programme of work, it is important to assess your organisation's state of readiness, which includes knowledge and awareness about FOI in addition to the current status of information and records management. Accurately ascertaining the degree to which the organisation is prepared for FOI and current approaches to IM is vital in order to produce a controlled and integrated plan of work.

Successful preparations will involve adequate information management, in addition to managed procedures for the release of information. Both of these elements of preparation may require supporting technical systems, particularly to manage the monitoring obligations adequately.

Preparing your information

There are already a number of excellent guides from a number of sources which provide guidance in this area (see Chapter 3, Useful References). However, FOI calls for a pragmatic approach to the way in which RM and IM should be implemented.

Without understanding the core concepts and organisational benefits of these areas, there is a possibility that any new policies implemented will meet FOI requirements alone without examining the information needs across the organisation. Indeed, without a good understanding of core business processes it is possible that a crisis response to FOI will result in less effective IM within your organisation.

It is also important to gauge how open your organisation is with information. For historical reasons, a traditional 'need to know' culture is likely to exist in many public sector organisations and it is as important to deal with cultural issues as well as the more tangible information itself.

Procedures for dealing with requests

This chapter is the main focus of the book, with one of the key requirements for compliance being to ensure that the processes for disclosing information are managed effectively. Although 20 working days may seem a relatively long period of time to provide information, the deadline will quickly pass if the request is mismanaged, there is uncertainty as to the location or format of information, it is difficult to retrieve or it is subject to exemptions. Depending upon the type of information you hold in your organisation, you may also require certain business knowledge or skills in order to assess exemptions and comply with a request.

This chapter also contains a section on publication scheme maintenance and how this can help reduce the resource implications of managing requests once FOI comes into force, and the duty to advice and assist applicants under FOI. Charging policies are also discussed briefly in this chapter.

Exemptions

While it is very important that organisations embrace the new culture of openness in order to comply with FOI, there will be instances where there is also a genuine need to withhold the information.

A number of exemptions exist under the Acts, but in order to be effective they must be consistently managed and applied and fully understood by those responsible for using them. Exemptions also require re-evaluation to ensure they remain applicable, which in turn will require adequate audit trails for any decisions taken.

This chapter contains a short section on the difference between the Data Protection Act 1988 and FOI. It also deals very briefly with the issue of confidentiality and third-party contracts in addition to assessment of 'public interest', a factor of some of the exemptions under FOI.

Audit trails and proving compliance

In order to prove compliance, organisations will need some method of centralised capture of information about requests to demonstrate their performance under FOI. Under codes of practice associated with both the Acts, there are requirements to capture certain statistics and further details are provided in this chapter. The way in which audit trails are approached will depend on the size and function of organisation, and to some extent, the number of requests. Any system that is implemented must be feasible in terms of being able to capture the data and resource implications. There may also be benefits to organisations in capturing data about requests and monitoring and reporting trends, and if so these requirements should be built into the system from the outset.

The chapter builds on issues discussed in the chapters on procedures for release and exemptions as both will require some kind of an audit trail in order to adequately to prove compliance.

Training

Training all staff to some degree will be essential as requests can be made to anyone in the organisation and do not have to mention FOI. The training programme has the potential to take a number of different forms depending both on the learning needs of staff and the state of readiness of organisation. Any programme should not forget the important cultural issues as well as management of information and records, which will be an important component of successful compliance.

Organisations should raise awareness of FOI and examine the role of everyone in the organisation in order to achieve compliance. Roles will depend upon a number of factors, including defined procedures for release of information (see Chapter 2 and also Chapter 4).

There will be a need for a continuous training programme, particularly if your organisation is likely to be affected by any case law. The turnover of staff also needs to be considered, with the construction of adequate induction programmes in order to maintain compliance with FOI.

Evaluating success and organisational benefits

In the absence of any case law prior to the implementation of FOI, the status of 'ready' becomes, in many ways, a moving target. What is important is that your organisation determines what factors will represent 'success', and that there is adequate flexibility in the approach to FOI to cater for any unforeseen requirements. Once compliance can be demonstrated, there will be a further opportunity to assess the benefits your programme of activities offers to your organisation. At this point you can also examine how these activities can be enhanced or modified to improve productivity or the effectiveness of business processes.

By many, this may seem like the 'nice to have' rather than essential. However, as discussed above, it is imperative that FOI preparations take into account the strategic view of IM to ensure there is not divergence between the IM and RM needs of the organisation, and plans for compliance with FOI.

Next steps

It is important that your organisation takes the appropriate steps to prepare for FOI, which should be relative to the current gaps existing in preparations, and the type and volume of information that you hold. It is also important to remember that different aspects of the preparations discussed in this book will be of different priorities to different organisations.

The next chapter will help you prioritise your programme of preparations, but it is very important to re-evaluate FOI priorities on a regular basis. As the date for full compliance comes ever closer, more information regarding expectations and interpretations of FOI is becoming available. This may affect the way in which your organisation prepares for FOI. Do not forget that preparations will continue to evolve after 1 January 2005, and it may be many months before the true implications of FOI for the public sector become more tangible. Consequently you need to ensure decisions regarding long-term strategies are factored into the initial preparation programme – enabling the actual implications of FOI to be more accurately quantified after 1 January 2005.

Where to start

Objectives

The objectives of this chapter are to enable you to:

- identify key issues that need to be addressed in order for your organisation to comply with FOI;
- understand some of the cultural aspects affecting your organisation and how they may influence preparations;
- plan an appropriate organisational structure that will facilitate the implementation of preparations.

Background

Adequate preparation will be one of the fundamental components of compliance. There are likely to be many different types of guidance relevant to this work, including that on project management to enable you to structure your plans and activities. Successful records management (RM) will also need to be an integral part of any plan for compliance, and both Acts have a code of practice on RM. These codes of practice include sections on responsibilities for RM, RM policies and also human resource requirements. Where applicable, this advice should be integrated with the issues below.

Before planning any programme of activities to achieve compliance, you should conduct a gap analysis. This analysis will determine the difference between what the legislation requires and what the organisation currently does in terms of information management (IM) and the provision of information. The exercise will require some basic knowledge of the Act and how implications will affect business conducted by the organisation.

The purpose of the gap analysis is to determine the tasks that need completing as part of the preparation programme. It is important to ensure that the availability of all components, such as staff and system requirements, in achieving these tasks are factored into your plans. Once all tasks have been identified it should then be possible to prioritise tasks in accordance with organisational needs and construct a programme to work towards compliance.

Prior to any action being taken, it will also be important to reflect on any current organisational strategies for IM, identifying opportunities for preparations to be integrated with current business initiatives. You may also wish to refer to Chapter 8 to start developing organisational goals and objectives for any FOI project or programme of activities.

Checklist

The checklist in this chapter is divided into three key areas. The first is general awareness of FOI and the implications it may have on your organisation; the next is regarding the structures that will be required in your organisation to achieve compliance; and finally there is a section on cultural issues. Some issues relating to IM are flagged in this chapter but are mainly dealt with in the following chapter.

Remember that not all of the issues below may be relevant to your organisation, and there are no right or wrong answers to many of the questions, including the supplementary questions. It is for you to decide what is most appropriate for your organisation, and how activities and tasks should complement one another throughout your preparation programme.

General awareness and understanding

Does your organisation have a basic understanding and appreciation of the appropriate Act?

With FOI potentially being able to change the way in which many public sector organisations conduct business, it is vital that everyone in your organisation has a basic understanding of the appropriate Act. In order to start assessing the preparations required, you may need to review all different aspects of business within your organisation to appreciate the full implications. Unless individuals throughout the organisation have an appreciation of the implications of FOI, preparations are unlikely to integrate effectively with existing business processes or address all issues required for compliance.

What approach to raising awareness would be most effective?

FOI will affect staff across your organisation in different ways. For example, some sections in your organisation may routinely produce sensitive material which is likely to continuously attract significant public interest. Conversely other areas may follow policy or adhere to procedures and controls that are widely understood and therefore attract little interest. How important is it that these differences are identified and factored into preparations from the outset?

What is the best way of raising general awareness of the majority of staff? There may be a number of media through which you are able to communicate basic facts about FOI such as newsletters, intranets, forums, presentations or more direct e-mails and visits to members of staff. Discussion groups may also be useful tool to involve a range of individuals from across the organisation.

One further consideration may be whether or not raising awareness should form part of an overall FOI training programme within your organisation. Apart from FOI possibly affecting all core and supporting business processes, requests for information can be made to anyone in the organisation and therefore staff must know how to process any request they receive. Training is discussed further in Chapter 7.

Do senior management appreciate the implications and potential risks and benefits?

If not, how will key implications be communicated to senior management? Often there will be organisational issues that more effective IM could help to resolve and these could be used to market FOI to management in the organisation. It is important to remember when approaching implications and potential risks that they are likely to be different for each level of management, perhaps even across departments, and any marketing should take this into account.

Before deciding on an approach, it would be worthwhile to look at previous issues that have been communicated to senior management teams in your organisations and evaluate the success of that communication. This should give you an indication of the most appropriate method of communicating with a range of staff across your organisation.

What information are you holding?

This question is mainly dealt with in the next chapter, but you should start thinking about your information, what it relates to and why it is held. Note that the Acts refer to information that is held and not to information that is owned. Should you be holding the third-party information that currently exists in your organisation? Should any programme to raise awareness also include those external to your organisation who provide you with information? The Acts are also fully retrospective and will therefore apply to any information held by your organisation, regardless of format, on 1 January 2005 and thereafter.

Do you know what the sources of your information are? Where third parties supply your organisation with information, to what extent they need to be aware of FOI? Involvement with third parties may also involve contractual issues which may need careful consideration (see Chapter 5). Please see the next chapter for further discussion on the RM and IM issues in your organisation.

What are your current communication channels with your potential customer groups?

A high-level assessment at the preparatory stage of who your customers may be and how you will communicate with them once FOI comes into force may assist with identification and prioritisation of tasks. What communication channels are already in place and with whom? How can these channels be best used to the benefit of both the customer group and your organisation leading up to and after 1 January 2005? It may be that communication channels need to be established with some groups and the most effective way of achieving this should be identified. Groups or departments within your organisation may already be in contact with these groups for business reasons, which may prove useful for FOI preparations.

Are any current functions within your organisation routinely involved in information provision?

This may influence a number of factors of preparation. What information do they currently deal with? Is the function suitable for dealing with all requests for information after 1 January 2005? How do they currently process requests? Will the processes they use need to be changed to ensure they are FOI compliant?

Are there circumstances where the function chooses not to disclose information? If so, how do they make decisions and record them? Are there examples of best practice that can be used in the formulation of any new procedures required for FOI?

Are there any other similar public sector organisations with which you can network?

There are already a number of FOI groups and forums throughout the UK which have been established by public sector bodies to share ideas about how best to prepare for the legislation. Membership of a network is likely to be highly beneficial, offering different approaches to compliance in addition to varying experience with information and records management. It will also facilitate the sharing of information which may include strategies, policies, and procedures, all of which will be useful to you when trying to formulate these documents for your own organisation.

In the absence of a UK benchmark, are there similar public sector organisations in other countries currently operating with FOI legislation?

These organisations may give you an indication of the levels of interest in your organisation and any new customer groups on the implementation of FOI. Making contact with these organisations may also prove useful to try to establish the most appropriate practice when dealing with requests and more successfully managing risk.

Organisational structures and systems

Who is responsible for FOI compliance?

Within your organisation, the chief executive or equivalent will ultimately be responsible for FOI, although he/she is likely to delegate responsibility to a specific area of the organisation or to an individual. Nomination of a specific post to take responsibility for compliance with FOI should be a high priority task if your organisation has yet to identify a suitable individual. An uncoordinated approach to tackling FOI will almost certainly result in non-compliance for most organisations.

Risks arising from content, accuracy and interpretation of information, in addition to current record-keeping procedures, may also inform the decision about who is to be given overall responsibility for the compliance programme. An awareness of these risks and how they should be managed should begin to form once people start to become aware of possible implications, which will vary across organisations.

It may also be useful to place some barriers around the remit of the FOI role, for example, IM, RM and possibly information security, which may feature heavily in the programme of preparation. Responsibilities for these areas and how they will contribute to the preparations should be agreed at the outset.

What resources are available or could be made available for preparations for FOI?

It is important to establish whether any additional resources will be made available for FOI both during the preparatory stage and after 1 January 2005. The resources available will affect the amount of work it is feasible to complete before the January deadline and also, potentially, in what order initiatives will be tackled.

Without any additional resources, tasks will have to be absorbed into existing roles and therefore may take longer or need to be broken down into smaller activities. Where this is the case, careful consideration needs to be given to how the initiatives will be managed, and also how tasks will be prioritised – taking into account existing workloads.

Absorbing many of the tasks required for FOI may not necessarily be a negative approach to compliance. Good business knowledge is likely to result in a more accurate assessment of the state of readiness in addition to procedures that comply with the legislation being more effectively integrated into existing business processes. You need to ensure that tasks have realistic timescales, which are negotiated with those involved prior to finalising any preparation programme.

Who will champion FOI throughout your organisation?

Successful initiatives usually require a champion. In the case of FOI, this should be someone who is able to understand the implications of the legislation and also able to convey the urgency and benefits of completing a preparations programme. Depending upon the size and structure of your organisation, it may be necessary to have more than one champion, particularly if you have a diverse range of roles and obligations with differing organisational needs.

Do you need to identify any other people that will help deliver the preparations? You may need to pilot various initiatives throughout your preparations and careful thought needs to be given to those chosen, particularly where timescales are short. Other roles will be essential in your programme and, taking into account the requirements of other aspects of compliance, you need to decide what these are and who is best suited to fill them.

How will you communicate progress on FOI initiatives?

Many of the questions above may help you formulate a list of those people with an interest in FOI preparations. Early decisions about what information people need to be kept informed, and how each group will be communicated to throughout the programme will both aid preparations and help maintain control of the preparations.

As the deadline for compliance draws nearer it is possible that some groups or departments in your organisation will construct their own plans for compliance if they are not fully informed of centralised or organisational approaches to compliance. Regular communications using a method appropriate for your organisation (as discussed previously) will also provide an opportunity for individuals to contribute to the programme and become more involved in preparations.

What systems do you have that currently facilitate information management?

At the preparation stage, you should not be attempting to establish technical solutions to respond to FOI requirements. There are many factors that could affect decisions about the appropriate solutions which, at the early stage of preparations, may be largely unknown. There are many aspects of compliance, some of which are discussed throughout this book, where either technical or manual solutions are possible. While technical solutions may have possible benefits of automation, better integration and consistency, cost may be a prohibitive factor where only a small number of requests are anticipated.

However, technical systems are likely to help manage compliance issues and it may be that systems that are currently used to manage information can be enhanced or changed in some way to partially meet some FOI requirements. It will therefore be useful to ascertain what systems are used throughout the organisation and how they are used to manage information. Issues to consider regarding technical solutions are further discussed in Chapters 4 and 5.

What are the main risks to your organisation?

What element of FOI presents these risks to your organisation? Non-compliance and the content of the information that may have to be placed in the public domain are likely to be two of the main considerations. However, there will be other risks and any that are assessed as having a high, detrimental impact should be managed by preparations from the earliest opportunity.

Every organisation is likely to have different risk areas that require managing and the topic of risk is frequently revisited throughout the subsequent chapters. Some additional risks that may need to be factored into the preparations for your organisation may be:

- Volume of requests: how many requests can your proposed structures cope with (see Chapter 4) and what will be the impact on business processes if the volume received exceeds this number?

- Justification of decision-making: do you have policies that document the rationale behind the way you work and any decision-making process in your organisation? Or do you have policies governing IM or RM that are not currently adhered to or are out of date? Justification for what information is and is not held on a particular issue may prove very difficult without policies that are enforced throughout the organisation.

- Inconsistent processing of requests arising from different information being released to the same request or exemption policies being inconsistently applied to the same information.

- Do you hold substantially similar information to another public body? If so, FOI may expose unexplained differences in information held and the way it is managed and used. This should also be a consideration when looking at what information should fall under an exemption, discussed in Chapter 5.

What are the organisational benefits?

FOI will offer benefits to all public sector organisations, although in reality they are unlikely to be realised by most until the key implications have had time to be adequately managed and controlled. The benefits of RM have long been voiced from information and records management sectors and are well documented in a number of sources. See the Useful References section at the end of this chapter for further information.

FOI provides an excellent opportunity to improve the credibility of public sector organisations, and to proactively welcome a wider input from the general public to decision-making processes and the way in which organisations operate. For further ideas on how to identify and develop benefits, see Chapter 8.

Can experience from previous projects be effectively used to plan FOI preparations?

FOI has the potential to affect every member of staff in your organisation; therefore, preparations should also be planned on an organisation-wide basis. Examining the success and lessons learnt from other projects on this scale should assist with preparations. There are a number of factors that could be examined, including the most effective means of communication, how to train staff, the speed at which initiatives are taken up by staff and also how to incorporate new requirements into existing working practices.

Cultural issues

Many of the initiatives or tasks required to achieve compliance may require a change in culture throughout your organisation, particularly if your organisation has traditionally operated as a 'need to know' organisation with regard to information. Addressing these types of issues from the outset is just as important as addressing each of the initiatives more directly associated with FOI. You may require a programme to specifically manage the necessary change in culture. However, you need to decide what is achievable in the time available and prioritise the issues where they are relevant to your organisation.

How willing is your organisation to make information available?

Is the concept of FOI actively encouraged in any area of your organisation? If so, are you able to apply the principles of openness in some groups or departments to others where openness is not encouraged?

Do you suffer from a 'blame culture'? Blame cultures often result in a lack of transparency or willingness to share information. FOI may be viewed as a means of providing more evidence or material to place blame for initiatives that, for whatever reason, have been deemed to 'fail'. It is imperative that organisations move away from this approach. FOI will lead to the exposure of information that has not previously been put into the public domain, and your organisation must decide how it is going to deal with this.

The current situation in some public sector organisations is a lack of transparency in how business is conducted, which can lead to a lack of public accountability. This is likely to change under FOI, as individuals in the public sector are likely to be held more accountable for actions and decisions taken. It is important that staff are aware of this; for some, it may provide the necessary motivation to change their working practices to meet new requirements.

What does FOI mean to your organisation in terms of culture, and what activities will need to be completed differently?

Accepting that information will need to be more proactively shared where appropriate under FOI is a vital element of realising many of the benefits. It will allow better information sharing and availability, both internally and externally, which could lead to a stronger culture of constructive collaboration, sharing and learning.

Engendering a culture of openness will also help to evaluate what information genuinely needs some protection under FOI and why. This could reduce the administrative burden in managing exemptions.

What are the barriers to the concept of transparency associated with FOI?

Do these differ to those that may exist for FOI preparations? How would these be best addressed in your organisation? Barriers to openness may be tangible or more cultural and intangible, and each barrier identified is likely to require a different course of action to address the issues it raises.

It is important to recognise that there may be some barriers, either physical or intangible, that are genuinely required to protect information. For example, appropriate technical and organisational measures are required to protect personal data under the Data Protection Act 1998, and failure to protect such information adequately is likely to constitute a breach under this Act. An appropriate balance is required; this is for your organisation to decide, taking into account the type of information you hold, and taking appropriate advice where necessary.

What is the organisational strategy for managing information?

A strong culture is likely to dictate to a certain extent any existing strategies for managing information, which may not have taken into account compliance with FOI when it was constructed and written. If your organisation has a strategy, it is essential that those responsible for delivering initiatives to comply with FOI discuss the way forward with those responsible for other aspects of IM, ensuring that FOI plans are not divergent from other IM initiatives.

Should your organisation not have an organisational strategy for managing information, it is essential to consider the information needs of business processes prior to implementing any initiatives solely for the purposes of complying with FOI. Without such consideration, preparations for FOI may be ineffective or even have a detrimental impact on existing business processes. You may also need to address informal IM activities and practices that are used in your organisation.

How integrated are IM initiatives across your organisation?

Size is often a core factor in a number of areas that are affected by the extent to which an organisation is considered integrated, but small organisations with substantially different functions can also appear to have limited integration. Where your organisation is disparate, for whatever reason, your plans for FOI will need to cater for this adequately. This issue is considered further in each of the following chapters.

At this stage, however, you need to decide the most appropriate way to take preparations forward. Should each unit make their own preparations for FOI? If so, what information will they need to manage any risks FOI may present to your organisation? In order to cope with FOI, are there any functions or information that should still be centralised? If so, can this be achieved within the time and budgetary constraints?

Summary

Having addressed the issues raised in this chapter, you should now have an understanding and appreciation of:

- issues that need to be addressed by your organisation to comply with FOI and the appropriate priority of tasks;
- implications and key risks for your organisation;
- current levels of understanding of the concepts of FOI throughout your organisation;
- resources available for compliance tasks, and how you will communicate progress on compliance with FOI with customer groups and staff;

- the possible nature and volume of requests that will be received from 1 January 2005.

Useful references

General

Each of the references below will provide you with some general information about the principles and concepts of FOI from a number of different viewpoints.

- Campaign for Freedom of Information: *http://www .cfoi.org.uk/*. The Campaign for Freedom of Information, Suite 102, 16 Baldwins Gardens, London EC1N 7RJ, England. Tel: 020 7831 7477, Fax: 020 7831 7461, E-mail: *admin@cfoi.demon.co.uk*.

- Guardian Online have two areas of their website that may be of interest. The first contains cases that have been in the news and supplementary information: *http://www .guardian.co.uk/freedom*. The second area has details about the various ways in which government information can be accessed: *http://politics.guardian.co.uk/foi*.

- Freedom of Information (FOI) Sites on the Internet website covers a wide range of countries that are already subject to FOI legislation: *http://www.law.utas.edu.au/ foi/bookmarks/FOI_index.html*.

- Office of the Irish Information Commissioner: *http:// www.oic.gov.ie/*.

- Open Government Canada Freedom of Information Coalition: *http://www.opengovernmentcanada.org/*.

- There are a number of public sector organisations that have started to place RM and IM policies, in addition to documents for FOI preparations, on their website. When looking to prepare any of these documents, conducting some searches on the Internet to see what material you are able to find may give you lots of examples to work with.

- The Constitution Unit at University College London offers a range of publications on FOI: *http://www.ucl .ac.uk/constitution-unit/foidp/publications.php*. Their telephone number is 020 7679 4977.

FOIA

- Department for Constitutional Affairs – the area of their website that is dedicated to FOI can be found at *http:// www.dca.gov.uk/foi/foidpunit.htm*. Their other contact details are: Department for Constitutional Affairs, Selborne House, 54–60 Victoria Street, London SW1E 6QW, England. Tel: 020 7210 8614.

- UK Information Commissioner: *http://www .informationcommissioner.gov.uk/* Information Commissioner's Office, Wycliffe House, Water Lane, Wilmslow, Cheshire SK9 5AF, England. Tel: 01625 545 745.

- National Archives: *http://www.nationalarchives.gov.uk/* The National Archives, Kew, Richmond, Surrey TW9 4DU, England. Tel: 020 8876 3444.

- Freedom of Information Act 2000, 2000 Chapter 36 – available from HMSO Online: *http://www.legislation .hmso.gov.uk/acts/acts2000/20000036.htm*.

- Explanatory notes to the Freedom of Information Act 2000, 2000 Chapter 36 – available from HMSO Online: *http://www.legislation.hmso.gov.uk/acts/en2000/2000en 36.htm*.

- A full list of those bodies covered by FOIA can be found at *http://www.dca.gov.uk/foi/coverage.htm*.

FOISA

- Scottish Information Commissioner – their contact details are: Kinburn Castle, Doubledykes Road, St Andrews, Fife KY16 9DS, Scotland. Tel: 01334 464610, Fax: 01334 464611, E-mail: *enquiries@itspublicknowledge.info*, *http://www.itspublicknowledge.info/*.

- Scottish Executive – the Scottish Executive has a dedicated section on its website. Their contact details are: Freedom of Information Unit, G-A North, Victoria Quay, Edinburgh EH6 6QQ, Scotland. Tel: 0131 244 5210, E-mail: *foi@scotland.gsi.gov.uk*, *http://www.scotland.gov.uk/Topics/Government/FOI*.

- National Archives of Scotland – their contact details are: Historical Search Room, HM General Register House, 2 Princes Street, Edinburgh EH1 3YY, Scotland. Tel: 0131 535 1334, Fax: 0131 535 1328, E-mail: *enquiries@nas.gov.uk*.

  West Search Room, West Register House, Charlotte Square, Edinburgh, EH2 4DJ, Scotland. Tel: 0131 535 1413, Fax: 0131 535 1411, E-mail: *wsr@nas.gov.uk*, *http://www.nas.gov.uk/*.

- Freedom of Information (Scotland) Act 2002, 2002 ASP 13 – available from HMSO Online: *http://www.scotland-legislation.hmso.gov.uk/legislation/scotland/acts2002/20020013.htm*.

- Explanatory notes to the Freedom of Information (Scotland) Act 2002, 2002 ASP 13 – available from HMSO Online: *http://www.scotland-legislation.hmso.gov.uk/legislation/scotland/en2002/2002en13.htm*.

Preparing your information

Objectives

The objectives of this chapter are to enable you to:

- identify the types of information you hold across your organisation;

- identify information that is likely to be of most interest once FOI comes into force and make specific plans to prepare that information;

- understand any risks your information may pose that require managing from an FOI perspective.

Background

The focus of this book is very much upon being able to process requests once FOI comes into force; however, this will not be possible to achieve without meeting the records management (RM) requirements that are associated with both the Acts. Each Act has a code of practice dedicated to RM: Section 46 under FOIA and Section 61 under FOISA.

There are already a number of excellent guides from a number of sources that provide guidance in this area, including both the National Archives and the National

Archives Scotland. Both also provide model action plans for achieving compliance with FOI, which are referenced at the end of this chapter.

However, as stressed in the previous chapter, one of the most important considerations in preparation is the RM and information management (IM) needs of the organisation, as well as for FOI. Without taking these into account, there is a danger that changes to cope with FOI will adversely affect the way in which information and records are used throughout core business processes. In order to be successful, it is essential to identify the most effective way in which to provide required information to business processes and then determine how FOI requirements can also be met.

As part of FOI preparations, there may be opportunities to review the information your organisation is holding and why – given the environment in which information is managed is constantly and rapidly changing. It is possible that information throughout the organisation could be rationalised or changed to meet business needs more appropriately. It is also important to gauge how open your organisation is with information and how willingly staff collaborate and share information.

One final consideration is that technology has significantly changed the way in which individuals have managed information over the past couple of decades. Staff in the majority of organisations have moved away from using corporate structures, typically defined by a registry-type function, to using their own on local or shared drives on personal computers.

A consequence of this shift in the way records are managed is that there are likely to be large numbers of files and folders only accessible to the individual who created them. Looking at the wider issue, staff have also now become accustomed to using their own filing systems and storage structures, and sharing their information only when required, rather than as a matter of routine.

Systems and methods used to file information and records may, therefore, be vastly different across the organisation, making it difficult to locate information in response to a request. The more distributed the storage of records, the more individuals will need to be involved in the location and retrieval of information to meet FOI obligations. There are likely to be many more issues affecting IM in your organisation and these should be teased out to identify any cultural changes that need addressing.

As stated at the beginning of this chapter, it is not the intention of this book to repeat guidance that is already available from a number of sources. What this checklist offers is some high-level, periphery questions that should allow the integration of RM and IM with other issues that need addressing to process requests under FOI.

Checklist

How does your organisation approach RM and IM?

RM and IM, traditionally viewed as different disciplines, are essential for compliance with FOI. However, with FOI covering all recorded information, it will be important to ensure various procedures and processes that are already in place for records incorporate or deal with recorded information.

You may choose to keep RM separate from IM, but it is very important to ensure that your organisation does not limit information provided to records when responding to a request. Two different approaches may also cause confusion for staff in terms of both processing requests and also complying with policies when processing information. This subject is addressed in more detail below.

Do your RM policies and procedures accommodate all 'recorded information'?

All recorded information will, in most organisations, be far more extensive than the 'records' held. It is important to identify the scope of recorded information, as some may not fall within the boundaries of RM in your organisation, and therefore could cause confusion after 1 January 2005 when requested. Once identified, it may also be important to incorporate recorded information into appropriate policies.

For example, are all drafts created in your organisation dealt with by your destruction policy? It is likely that only the final version of any document created becomes a record and it is the record that is listed in any policy you may have. In addition to drafts, other recorded information also requires consideration such as handwritten notes, for example, those made during a tendering process; CCTV and all other video and audio tape recordings; text messages and telephone answering machine messages. It is possible that your organisation already has policies for some of this material, but it should be ensured these are documented, particularly retention and destruction, to enable justification of why material has been destroyed.

If your organisation does not have a policy to control and manage this type of recorded information, there may be inconsistency both in what is released, and possibly in decisions about what can be released. A lack of policies may also lead, in some cases, to accusations of purposely destroying material, which should clearly be avoided at all costs. You may need to consider whether retention and destruction procedures are sufficient for information you hold that does not go on to become a 'record', or whether this will be dealt with in separate guidance to staff in your organisation.

To what extent does your organisation currently comply with the RM code of practice in the appropriate legislation?

Both codes of practice set out RM requirements in order to achieve compliance with FOI. Records management must be a priority task for compliance but it is also important to ensure that adequate groundwork is completed to ensure any new initiative can be sustained once FOI comes into force. For further information, see Useful References at the end of this chapter.

What skills do you have in house to deal with IM and RM issues?

Whether or not your organisation currently meets the standards set out in the RM codes of practice, it is important to ascertain what skills you will need to continue managing recorded information after 1 January 2005. Furthermore, while successful RM will go a long way towards preparing your organisation's information, it must be remembered that the Acts refer to information. IM and RM do require different skill sets and therefore you need to decide which skill set is appropriate for your organisation given the types of information and records held, and for what purpose they are held.

Training of staff in IM and RM will also be essential for compliance, as will ensuring everyone has an understanding of the concept of FOI and how it will affect them. It is also important to highlight to staff the importance of the role they play in any corporate RM and IM strategy and policy, including how to manage corporate information. This issue is dealt with in more detail in Chapter 7.

What information are you holding?

It is likely that your organisation will have to make some IM preparations in order to comply with FOI. Many organisations have followed the advice of the Model Action Plans produced by the National Archives and the National Archives of Scotland (see Useful References at the end of this chapter), undertaking an information audit. In order to be fully prepared for FOI, it is essential that you are aware of what information you are holding, where it is, and how it can be accessed and retrieved. It would also be useful to know whether there are any types of information that may require extra preparation: for example, material that may be exempt from FOI. Exemptions are discussed in more detail in Chapter 5.

You will also need to be aware of the different types of information you may be holding to ensure you comply with the appropriate legislation. In addition to FOI, you still need to comply with the Data Protection Act 1998 which broadly speaking governs the processing of personal data, and the Environmental Information Regulations for environmental information. Each of these has different requirements, governing the way in which information should be released or made available and it is important to ensure your organisations does not inadvertently breach one of the pieces of legislation in an effort to comply with another. This issue is further addressed in the next chapter.

How is your organisation structured and how does this relate to information flows?

The structure of your organisation and information flows may affect a number of elements of preparation: the way in which you train people; the positioning of FOI 'experts' throughout the organisation: the way in which information is made available and the procedures for processing requests are some examples. It will also be a factor in any IM and RM policies that are implemented.

The business processes and the way in which they are completed across your organisation may also provide a valuable 'top-down' link to the information used by staff across your organisation. The more comprehensively you are able to map the existence of information, the easier it should be to process the request once FOI comes into force.

It is also important to identify where information flows between your organisation and a third party. Where your information is shared, it may be duplicated and therefore also held by a third party. This issue is dealt with in a number of questions discussed below.

Constructing a comprehensive picture of information and records can be extremely time consuming and it may be that all these issues are incorporated into an information audit. However, it is likely to be an extremely important activity. You will need to decide what priority this task should have in order to ensure compliance with FOI by 1 January 2005.

Do you know what information is in your archives?

While this may seem like a relatively simple and straight-forward question, how certain can you be that archiving policies have been strictly followed? If you are uncertain as to what is in your archives, they may present a risk to you in terms of non-compliance and resources required to retrieve information once the Acts come into force. You may also need to ensure that procedures for retrieving information from archives will allow your organisation to comply with FOI, in particular, the 20 working-day time limit.

What information belonging to your organisation is held by third-party organisations?

Remember that FOI refers to information you hold and not information you own. There may be a large volume of your information that is held by a third-party organisation, where the third party is also subject to FOI. This should be taken into account throughout preparations, particularly when applying exemptions, as discussed in the next chapter.

With the implementation of FOI it is still important to ensure that information sharing and collaboration is achieved in a controlled manner, and for legitimate business purposes. While FOI should not prevent the sharing of information where it contributes to improve organisational efficiency and effectiveness, care should be taken to ensure that those with whom information is to be shared understand any exemptions you intend to apply.

One of the keys to successful compliance and managing risk to reputation will be controlling the publication of material. If you wish to apply exemptions to your information under FOI, you must ensure that information is not placed in the public domain by an uncontrolled source. This is discussed further in Chapter 5.

What information do you hold that is owned by a third party?

Similarly, developing the issues raised above, some of the information your organisation is holding may belong to a third party, which may substantially complicate procedures for making that information available. This information could belong to another organisation subject to FOI, but it is also possible that it will belong to an organisation that is not subject to the legislation. If you are holding information, it is subject to FOI: how will you deal with requests for information that belong to an organisation not subject to FOI?

It is extremely important to ensure that your organisation is holding only information where it is required for business purposes and not documents that are 'nice to have'. All information held should also comply with IM and RM policies. This and the previous question are revisited in Chapter 5.

It should be noted that FOI is unlikely to apply to information you are holding on behalf of a third party. If this applies to information you hold, you should check the relevant Act carefully, taking advice as appropriate as to whether or not FOI applies.

How static or dynamic is your information?

An information audit should tell you what you are holding in terms of records and information. It may also be useful to try and ascertain how often your types of records change. Information is likely to continuously change or be generated at the working level, but providing it falls into a record type that has already been planned for under FOI, it can be treated as all the other information in that particular type.

However, if your organisation is continually generating new types of records and information that need to be reviewed for possible exemptions under FOI, you will need processes that can cope with constant change. One example is a regular review of the retention and destruction policy to ensure new record types are catered for.

Does your organisation have existing information security and classification policies? Will they be compliant with FOI?

Some organisations may have previously used classifications for information to flag sensitivity or potential embarrassment that the information may cause to either themselves or a third party. This cannot be a consideration under FOI in most circumstances. You may therefore need to reassess how these classifications are applied to documents and also how you will process requests for information containing any existing markings. Staff throughout your organisation may need to be aware that existing markings are not FOI compliant and steps should be taken to ensure requests are processed in accordance with the relevant legislation.

How well do you know your customer's information needs?

How do your customers currently access your information? Do you think this will continue or will the requirement change after 1 January 2005? How well have you consulted with potential FOI customer groups? If you are aware what is likely to be of interest, in advance of 1 January 2005, you may be able to prepare key information that you know will be requested. Using this information, you may also be able to predict more accurately the volume of requests that you will receive as the predicted volume may affect any arguments put to senior management regarding resourcing of FOI and systems support.

Do you hold information that may be of interest to certain groups?

Has this information previously been available or withheld from publication? Again, this area is discussed further in the next chapter, but the volume of information that you are holding that is of interest to others will help you determine what may be requested and the potential volume of requests.

Summary

Having addressed the issues raised in this chapter, you should now have an understanding and appreciation of:

- a plan of action to construct inventories of information and records that exist throughout your organisation;
- the type and volume of information that exists in your organisation;
- information held by your organisation is likely to be of interest under FOI.

Useful references

General

- BS ISO 15489-1, The British Standard on Records Management.

- How to complete a survey of records and information, available from the National Archives: *http://www .nationalarchives.gov.uk/recordsmanagement/advice/pdf/ best_complete_survey.pdf.*

- There are a range of organisations that offer information audits and related information management services, which you should find by searching the Internet. There are also an increasing number of tool kits offered to enable you to conduct your own in-house audits, which again can be found by searching the Internet.

FOIA

- Lord Chancellor's Code of Practice on the Management of Records Issued under Section 46 of the Freedom of Information Act 2000 – available from the Department of Constitutional Affairs (DCA): *http://www.dca.gov.uk/foi/ codemanrec.htm.* See Chapter 2 for full contact details of the DCA.

- There is a range of model action plans available from the National Archives: *http://www.nationalarchives.gov.uk/ policy/foi/default.htm.* See Chapter 2 for full contact details of the National Archives.

- The Information Commissioner's Office (ICO) has made a range of Awareness Guidance available. At the time of this book going to print, there were 13 in the series. One of the series is on records management frequently asked questions: *http://informationcommissioner.gov.uk/.* For full contact details of the ICO, please see Chapter 2.

FOISA

- Freedom of Information (Scotland) Act 2002 Code of Practice on Records Management, November 2003 – available from the Scottish Executive: *http://www.scotland.gov.uk/about/FCSD/MCG-NW/00-018022/s61code.pdf*. See Chapter 2 for full contact details of the Scottish Executive.

- Model Action Plan available from the National Archives of Scotland (NAS): *http://www.nas.gov.uk/miniframe/foi/PDF/map.pdf*. See Chapter 2 for full contact details of the NAS.

4

Procedures for dealing with requests

Objectives

The objectives of this chapter are to enable you to:

- begin to construct procedures for dealing with requests across your organisation;
- examine the periphery activities that may be associated with releasing information and determine how these will be dealt with in your organisation;
- begin to devise a long-term strategy for the most appropriate means of making information held by your organisation publicly available.

Background

One of the key obligations under FOI is responding to requests for information. Reacting within the legal constraints governing the processing of requests for information will be fundamental to compliance. Both Acts have a time limit of 20 working days in which organisations must respond to a request. This limit will be quickly reached if: the request is mismanaged; there is uncertainty as to the location or format of information; information is difficult to retrieve or is subject to exemptions.

The provision of information will depend upon good information management (IM) and records management (RM) in addition to processes that ensure all of the activities needed to process requests are completed within 20 days. In some cases, responses may be very simple; however, depending upon the type of information you hold and the structure of your organisation, requests may also be extremely complex involving a large number of staff.

This chapter also examines the need to make strategic considerations as to how information should be placed in the public domain. Areas discussed include publication scheme maintenance and the effective use of any other communications media your organisation has for providing information to the general public – such as your website.

Checklist

This is the most extensive checklist contained in this book and is divided into three sections. The first looks at the procedures for dealing with requests. There are subtle differences between the two Acts with regard to processing requests, which are highlighted throughout. There are also further interpretations of the requirements of the Acts that should help you with implementing appropriate procedures.

The next section examines which periphery tasks also need to be integrated into your procedures; the final section looks at the need for consideration at a strategic level. This section looks at procedures to continually improve the way in which you make information available with a view to minimising resource implications.

Procedures for the release of information

Who will decide what legislation is applicable to any request made?

One of the first tasks that must be completed on receipt of a request for information is to determine which legislation is applicable to a specific request, assuming it is a valid request. If the request is for personal data of which the applicant is the subject, the person making the request will need to submit a Subject Access Request (SAR) under the Data Protection Act 1998 (DPA). If the information being requested is environmental information, it will fall under the Environmental Information Regulations (EIRs). Although the EIRs are broadly similar to FOI in terms of obligations placed on organisations when processing requests, there are differences and you will need to ensure your organisation puts measures into place that ensure compliance with both. Finally, if the request is for information that does not constitute a SAR and is not for environmental information, it will be governed by FOI.

Do you have the necessary knowledge in your organisation to be able to differentiate between the legislation? To what extent will you ensure your staff are aware of the differences between the legislation? What measures will you put in place to ensure compliance with the different legislation?

What will your organisation deem a valid request under FOI?

Under FOI, there are number of criteria that need to be fulfilled in order for the request for information to fall under the legislation. These are discussed in more detail in the codes of practice under Section 45, FOIA and Section 60, FOISA. In summary, the request must be in writing (or another format that can be referenced under FOISA), and contain contact details and the request for information.

However, the request does not need to be responded to if it is vexatious or if it is a repeat request (an identical or substantially similar request from the same person within a reasonable time period), or if responding would exceed the upper cost threshold. While these may be useful exceptions to note, it is likely that some record of the original request and actions taken should still be recorded, and therefore you may also choose to include them in any procedures that are devised. Furthermore, you may also need to devise policies to ensure applicants are fairly treated for any issues that are not specifically dealt with by the legislation. One example is the length of time within which a request is considered a repeat request and another would be your organisation's definition of 'vexatious'.

How can your organisation receive requests?

Before trying to identify the different ways in which requests may be made to your organisation, it is worth noting that there is a subtle difference in the two Acts in terms of how a request can be made. FOIA states that a request must be in writing and then sets a number of conditions for the text of such a request. FOISA states that a request should in writing or 'in another form which, by reason of its having some permanency, is capable of being used as a subsequent reference'.

Consequently, this implies that those requests made to authorities operating under FOISA may be legitimately made using a more diverse range of media. Any system used to manage or track requests must be able to initiate any processes used to respond, regardless of how the request is received. However, organisations under both Acts should also be mindful of obligations they have under the Disability Discrimination Act 1995 (DDA). You need to ensure that any processes developed to deal with requests do not result in somehow making your information inaccessible.

Taking into account requests can be made to anyone in the organisation, requests could be made in e-mail or by letter and do not have to make reference to FOI. How will you ensure that every request for information is identified? How will staff recognise requests and know how to deal with them? Are there any types of request that staff should deal with at the point of entry to the organisation? If so, how will you ensure these requests are dealt with in the 20-day time limit?

How will staff know whether or not they have the authority to process a request? Are staff aware of the different legislation governing the information you hold? How will FOI be balanced with the need to maintain information security across your organisation? This is especially pertinent where requests are likely to be dealt with at the point of entry to the organisation. It will be vital that staff are aware of their obligations under FOI and how these may relate to previous classifications relating to information security (which was discussed in the previous chapter).

Where appropriate, you would probably not want to prevent staff from processing requests for information that are already dealt with routinely. However, do you know where information already flows to and from in your organisation? How is this managed and who has authority to make information available? Examining existing processes may give you some ideas on how to take forward requests under FOI and highlight the most appropriate practice for your organisation. Where information is currently made available, you may decide that you still need to incorporate this into any tracking system implemented, and this is discussed further below.

It is important at this stage to consider any customer enquiry functions that already exist throughout your organisation. These functions are likely to receive requests that relate to FOI. They may also provide examples of the most appropriate way to deal with requests for information, as they will use certain procedures for dealing with these requests. Finally, they may also play a formal role in dealing with FOI, and therefore need to be incorporated into the preparations.

Do you need to develop new procedures for capturing information about requests?

Any request for information will fall under FOI, providing it is made in writing (FOIA) or in a format that can be referenced (FOISA). The only other details that your organisation can legitimately request are contact details (a name and address for correspondence, which can include e-mail) and a description of the information requested. Your organisation does have a duty to advise and assist an applicant and as part of that duty, you may ask for clarification from the applicant about the information requested in order to enable your organisation to identify and locate it.

However, you cannot insist on collecting any information from the applicant regarding why they want the information or how they will use it. There may be legitimate circumstances where asking these types of questions enable you to more easily identify locate the information requested by the applicant. Although you may ask these types of questions, it should be made clear to the applicant why you are asking and that they are not obliged to answer should they not wish to do so.

All of the activities described above may need to be captured and recorded in order to provide an audit trail of how a request was processed. Once you know what information you will generate about a request, you need to make a decision about what you want or need to capture and how this can be achieved. These issues are further discussed under the tracking and monitoring questions below.

What activities will be required in order to process requests for information?

Prior to deciding how requests will be dealt with, all the activities necessary to complete a request should be identified. In order to achieve this it may be useful to look at the first subsection of the first section of both Acts, which provide the fundamental elements of FOI. FOIA, Section 1 states:

> 1 (1) Any person making a request for information to a public authority is entitled –
>
> (a) to be informed in writing by the public authority whether it holds the information of the description specified in the request, and
>
> (b) if that is the case, to have that information communicated to him.

Under FOIA, the duty outlined at subsection (1)(a) is referred to as 'the duty to confirm or deny'. In some respects FOISA is far simpler in terms of basic requirements. FOISA states:

> 1(1) A person who requests information from a Scottish public authority which holds it is entitled to be given it by the authority.

There is no duty to confirm or deny information is held under FOISA. Both of the sections stated above are subject to exemptions under their respective Acts, which for FOIA include exemptions from the duty to confirm or deny. These are discussed in more detail in the next chapter.

Once you understand what activities will be required to enable you to meet your obligations under the legislation, you can then begin assigning tasks, and determine the most appropriate way in which to deal with requests. There is already some information available on activities which is available from the Department of Constitutional Affairs website, referenced at the end of this chapter.

Will you process requests in a centralised or distributed manner?

A fully centralised function means that all requests will come into a central repository and be dealt with by a dedicated team of individuals, who will also manage the request during the lifecycle of activities that you have identified above. A centralised function could be real or virtual, connected by a system that all members of the centralised function can access and control. The option at the other end of the spectrum is a fully distributed function, where requests are managed to resolution by a large number of staff across the organisation, possibly at the request's point of entry to the organisation. Using this option, there would be no central management or coordination of requests for information.

In reality, most organisations are likely to employ methods of response that have properties of both a distributed and centralised function, with the choice being influenced by identified risks, resources and systems available to cope with FOI. Decisions about response mechanisms need to take into account a number of factors based both on the size and structure of your organisation, the nature of the information you hold and the anticipated number of requests. If you have already gone through the previous chapters you may already have some ideas about how to structure your response processes.

Using a basic knowledge of your organisation, are both of these options feasible? What are the advantages and disadvantages of each option? This question should be considered from both the logistical perspective of processing requests and also from an information perspective. The information perspective should consider where information is held and what business knowledge is required to locate and retrieve information, and process requests.

Will a central unit or post conduct all processing necessary to respond to a request, or will some activities need to be completed by individuals throughout the organisation? You may need business knowledge for certain activities within the process, such as assessing the application of exemptions.

Do staff in your organisation have access to common information sources? If so, some degree of centralisation may be required to ensure consistency in the information placed in the public domain. Conversely, if all information sources are distributed with no common means of access, processing requests will need to be distributed to some degree, as there are no common information sources that can be accessed by a central function. Therefore, some activities involved in responding to a request will have to be distributed to at least a representation of those able to access each source of information.

What resources will be available to help process requests and how will they be coordinated? Once you have determined the optimum solution you need to ascertain whether it can be adequately resourced. If resources are limited, it may be that the processing needs to be completed in a distributed manner and integrated into existing posts in an effort to disseminate resource requirements. However, the implications of this approach on core business processes should be fully thought through.

As discussed in the previous chapter, do you have information that may be of particular interest after FOI? If so, is the team, department or group that hold that information resourced to deal with FOI requests? What advice and guidance will they require and what will the training requirements be? Training is dealt with in more detail in Chapter 7. Finally, regardless of the way in which requests are processed, you will have a need to capture certain information about requests, which is discussed below.

How will you determine whether you hold information and then retrieve it?

If you have read the previous two chapters, you should have started to build up a picture of the type of information that exists in your organisation and the interest it may attract. It is possible that you already have satisfactory RM procedures across your organisation and are confident where records are held, but remember that FOI applies to all recorded information.

In addition to taking into account record stores, you may need different procedures to find information or consider other sources that perhaps are not regarded as records. For example, what will your organisation's policy be on e-mails? Unless people regularly place e-mails in an electronic document or records-management system, inboxes and permanent filing systems within e-mail accounts will technically become sources of organisational information. This particular issue requires careful consideration as there may be data protection issues.

Are there any systems that you can put in place in the time available that will facilitate the tasks of locating and retrieving information? It may be that a short-term measure is to form a network of staff with good business knowledge that can help in the location of material. However, this method will only be as good as the knowledge the staff hold, and is unlikely to be sustainable for any length of time, especially if your organisation receives a high volume of requests. Using this method may also result in a detrimental impact on an individual's role and the contributions they make to core business processes, which must be considered when deciding on the best approach.

Do you have a separate duty to confirm whether or not the information is held?

This duty is specifically related to FOIA and does not exist for authorities governed by FOISA. If this requirement does apply to your organisation, what activities will you need to undertake in order to satisfy your obligations? Will you need to review the information being requested before you are able to make a decision whether you need to confirm whether or not the information is held?

Who will decide whether or not this duty applies and what policies will be required to ensure decision making is consistent? How will you record any decisions so that they can be audited and are available for any future requests for the same information?

Your organisation may have certain record types where you believe you are exempt from this duty. If so, it could be useful to write any policies accordingly and incorporate any information needed to comply with FOI into the creation stage of the document, where possible, for example, using document classification systems.

Who will decide whether an exemption is applicable?

This question is mainly dealt with in the next chapter but it is important to decide who should have the ultimate authority to decide when an exemption is applicable. This may be delegated or controlled by a single individual, depending upon what is most appropriate for your organisation. Many of the considerations are likely to be the same as those stated in the above question. What activities will be required in order to assess the application of an exemption to information? Will you need to review each individual piece of information before making decisions about exemptions?

Many of the exemptions are subject to the public interest test (often termed *qualified exemptions* under FOIA). How will you assess and record public interest? Factors that affect your decisions are subject to change and therefore it is important to keep an accurate record of what decisions were made at any particular time and how different factors influenced that decision. This activity may also be time consuming. Under FOIA, the 20 working-day time limit can be reasonably extended to allow consideration of the public interest, but this provision does not exist under FOISA.

Will you go out to consultation when processing requests for information? The information may belong to a third party and the codes of practice recommend that they are consulted where possible. If your policy will be to consult third parties, you need to ensure that the consultation period is started early enough within your 20-day deadline to ensure compliance.

What will your policies be on making information available in alternative formats?

Twenty days to process a request for information is not a long time, particularly if a request is complex, needs to be collated from disparate information sources and is subject to exemptions. Therefore, policies on how you will make information available may help those processing requests cut down on the time required to go through potentially lengthy decision-making processes.

Under FOI, applicants may express a preference for the format of the response, which should generally be accommodated where practicable. Do you know in which formats you are able to provide information? How readily can information be converted into an alternative format if it cannot be made available in the format in which it exists? Do you have information in your organisation that exists in an obsolete or inaccessible format and therefore would have to be converted to an alternative format before it could be made available? How are you going to deal with your obligations under the DDA in terms of providing information in alternative formats?

An alternative format may also reduce the cost implications, thereby making information more accessible to applicants and easier for your organisation to process. For example, a lengthy document could be made available from the organisation's website rather than provided as a photocopy, reducing the resource implications for the organisation and also the cost implications for the applicant.

How will you respond to refusals?

How will you decide when a request for information will be refused (when it is not a valid request or for information that is exempt)? Who will respond to the applicant? What information will you record about refusals? How will you record this information? Do you need to develop templates for this activity? Templates may prove useful for ensuring all applicants are treated consistently and that you include all necessary information in a refusal letter. Both the Acts require certain information to be communicated to the applicant under these circumstances and using templates may be one way of ensuring your organisation meets its obligations.

Are you likely to have partial refusals, with information being redacted where it is exempt within documents? How will you record what information is exempt? Again, you may want templates to consistently deal with partial refusals. You will also need some mechanism in place to capture what information was placed in the public domain, where information has been changed or amended for the purposes of publication.

How will you track requests?

Do you know what volume of requests for information is currently processed by your organisation? Do you think that the number of requests for information will increase after 1 January 2005? Do you have an existing system to track these requests? If not, how will you ensure compliance with the 20 working-day time limit?

Proving compliance without some means of tracking requests may prove extremely difficult. The greater the number of requests, the more difficult it is likely to be to ensure your organisation is compliant with FOI and also coordinate the disclosure of information.

In order to make adequate preparations for FOI, it is important to make some kind of estimation of the number of requests you are likely to receive. You should assess any risks that the estimated number of requests is likely to present to your organisation and decide on the most appropriate means of tracking requests. You may also want to consider making contingency plans in the event of the number of requests being significantly different than anticipated.

It is likely that the larger the anticipated volume of requests, the greater the need for your organisation to have automated tracking. It may be that a type of workflow option is most appropriate, but this will also depend upon how and where you store your recorded information, and who is able to access it. Automated prompts and reporting facilities may also be useful, and any user or system requirement that is developed should take into account the monitoring obligations detailed in the question below.

How will requests be monitored?

There are obligations under both the Acts contained in the codes of practice that require organisations to report statistics, including instances where part or all of the information was withheld. The FOIA Code of Practice issued under Section 45 also requires information to be kept for senior managers to ensure 'cases are being properly considered, and whether the reasons for refusal are sound'.

Under FOISA, the draft code of practice under Section 60 (5) of the Act has set out what has to be monitored, which are:

- requests that have been refused and the reasons for refusal;
- fees which have been charged for processing requests;
- reviews that have been carried out;
- instances where the time limit for reply has been exceeded and reasons.

While neither of the Acts or associated codes of practice require organisations to capture information about all requests they receive, the requirements listed above may require a holistic approach to capturing information about requests – rather than just dealing with the statistics specified.

Given the requirements of the Acts, what information about requests is it feasible to capture? Will this meet all the requirements laid out in the Acts and the codes of practice? How will you ensure that the information can be collated and reported? How can you be sure that all requests that should be monitored will be?

Furthermore, once you have addressed the legal perspective, you may also need to think about how you will prove compliance. What information do you need to capture about a request in order to ensure actions can be adequately audited during any complaints or review process? Should an applicant remain dissatisfied after a review or complaint, will the information captured stand up to scrutiny by the appropriate commissioner? See Chapter 6 for more details.

What systems do you have that could facilitate tracking and monitoring requests?

Automation of tracking may reduce resource implications and also provide a more rigorous audit trail for any requests. However, any supporting system must be able to support the processes for responding to requests regardless of who completes each activity. This will be relatively simple if your organisation is small and dealing with requests is fully centralised. However, if dealing with information requests has a degree of distribution in various locations, supporting system design could be necessarily more complex.

Who needs to be able to access the tracking system? Does there need to be an overall controller who is responsible for monitoring requests? Can the system automate any elements of the process you have defined to deal with information requests? How will you hold information about what has been placed in the public domain? What information about requests do you want to hold in the system?

All of these questions could affect the functionality of any chosen system, although your organisation may already have something that offers some of the functionality required. Does your organisation need to develop a new system or is there an existing system that could be used?

What level of investment or cost can you justify without an accurate forecast of the number of requests you are likely to receive? Can you implement a new system or required system changes before 1 January 2005? If not, what will you do as an interim measure? A manual solution is only likely to be feasible with a small number of requests to manage, where they will be processed in a centralised manner.

What risks are posed to your organisation in the processing of requests?

You may have already started to build a picture of the risks FOI poses to your organisation, and the processing of requests may help minimise them to some extent. In addition to non-compliance with FOI, there may be sensitive or contentious subject matter contained in the information placed in the public domain.

Are there any obvious risks you need to manage that are associated with your information? Can you put any extra activities into the processing of requests that will help manage and minimise the risks identified? Some of the risks that are likely to be more common are discussed further in some of the questions below.

How important is it for staff to know what information has been placed in the public domain?

This effectively represents a feedback loop to those in your organisation, which will keep staff informed of what information has been placed in the public domain. Information held by your organisation may not be deemed sensitive or contentious but if it is, or it is likely to be of public interest, it could be beneficial to keep key staff aware of information that has been disclosed.

What could happen if your staff are not aware of what information is in the public domain? If the effects are minimal, you may not require this stage of the process. However, if the effects are likely to be significant, who needs to know what has been placed in the public domain? Are they already part of the process for making information available? If they are not part of the process, they may require access to additional information that was taken into consideration when making a decision, such as factors that influenced the public interest test.

In some circumstances, it could be important to disseminate information about what has been released to staff in your own organisation or to third parties with which you regularly work. How will staff be kept informed about what information has been placed in the public domain? How will you keep third parties involved?

Depending upon the business of your organisation, it may be essential that the approach to responding is an integrated input from all those teams that may hold relevant information, to ensure the response represents the organisational view.

It may also be necessary to keep the media or press relations staff involved in processing requests. Some information being placed in the public domain may attract substantial public interest and subsequent risks need to be managed. Remember, without knowing details about what information is being given to whom or for what purpose the information will be used, all responses may carry the same risk in terms of publicity or the potential effects on organisational reputation.

Therefore, how will you keep all necessary teams involved? What input do teams need to have to the response process? How will you set up communications across your organisation after FOI comes fully into force?

How important is it to ensure consistency in information released?

Again, the answer to this question may lie in some of the responses to questions in the previous chapter, but it may be that you have a vast number of departments across your organisation, all of which deal with totally different types of information. Therefore, while there maybe a need to ensure consistency in the way requests are handled, the need will not be so great to ensure consistency in the information placed in the public domain.

However, where you have a number of departments that process the same type of information, it will be vital that they all have the same approach to what information will be made available, and also how exemptions will be applied. Inconsistencies will cause dissatisfaction among applicants and are likely to be extremely difficult to justify. This may result in complaints to the organisation, or even to the appropriate commissioner.

Periphery tasks

What will be your policy on charging?

The charging policy implemented by your organisation may provide a means of recouping some of the costs FOI will bring to your organisation. The charging regimes under FOIA and FOISA differ slightly and it is important to ensure you are aware of what you are able to charge under the Act. It is also important to ensure that if you have different charging policies for your publication scheme and processing requests, staff are aware how they differ and when each policy should be used.

How will your charging policy be implemented?

If your organisation has decided to charge for the provision of information, you need to decide who will manage the charging processes and policies. Will costs be calculated by those processing the requests or by a separate function? How will you invoice applicants for the information?

Will you want to record costs in the same system you use to capture requests? It may be beneficial to capture this information in the same system, as information does not have to be made available to the applicant until the payment is received. Furthermore, the time period between issuing an invoice or notice of fees to the applicant and receiving payment is excluded from the 20-day time period. It may, therefore, be useful to have all the information relating to a particular request in the same system in case of future queries or issues about the way in which a request was processed.

Who will monitor requests that are outstanding and waiting for payment? Who will ensure that when payments are received, the request is processed to completion? Who will be responsible for closing requests where an applicant was notified of costs and no payment was ever received?

How will you ensure consistency in charging?

You need to be certain that any charging policy is consistently applied, meaning that regardless of how many people request the same set of information, each applicant is charged the same cost to access it. This may be particularly difficult if you chose to process requests in a distributed manner. Without a central system for capturing information about costs of providing information, it is highly unlikely you can be certain of, or prove, consistency.

How will you fulfil your obligations to advise and assist enquirers?

This question should be a consideration for all activities within the processes required for compliance with FOI.

Handling initial enquiries effectively may reduce the number of requests for information that enter the formal processing procedures, particularly if the information requested is already in the public domain.

However, before you decide what role your staff will play, and therefore what activities they should undertake, you must also consider what it is reasonable for them to know and complete in terms of activities. Do the majority of staff know what information is held by your organisation? Will staff be able to easily determine what organisational information is already in the public domain? Given that requests can be made to anyone in the organisation, are all staff aware of FOI and how they should handle enquiries and requests for information?

Also, you should not forget any obligations you may have under Environmental Information Regulations (EIRs). If you hold environmental information, this will fall under the EIRs and can therefore be requested verbally. This may mean that staff need to be aware of what information they need to obtain from enquirers or applicants when a request is made verbally to ensure your organisation is then able to meet its legal obligations.

Long-term considerations

Would there be any benefit to your organisation in identifying trends?

Does your organisation have a high profile or a customer base whose information needs are highly dynamic? Do you need to rapidly respond to changing information requirements? Would requests for information of a particular subject signal a potential problem to your organisation? Are you anticipating a large volume of requests?

If you responded positively to any of the above questions, it could be beneficial to your organisation to monitor trends in requests for information. First, what do you need to monitor? Can you use subject or title, or do you need to somehow classify the request, perhaps with keywords? This may help with more accurate trend analysis if you have information that could be requested by applicants using a number of different terms.

How frequently do you need to monitor trends and which teams would benefit from this type of information? Depending on core business processes and the type of information that your organisation holds, there may be other benefits that trend analysis could offer. Key people in your organisation who deal with customers or the media may be able to offer some further advice about this particular issue.

Having identified information about requests that may be of value and decided which trends your organisation wants to monitor, you should then look more closely at the data you will need to collect and how resource-intensive the production of statistics might be. You should avoid generating statistics without reason and ideally undertake some type of analysis of the benefits against cost (which may be in terms of number of hours work required) to ensure you can effectively use all the information you have spent time and effort collecting.

What will your policies be for routine publication?

Information made available in the publication scheme is exempt from FOI as it is 'otherwise accessible'. The scheme therefore offers an excellent opportunity to reduce the resource implications of FOI after 1 January 2005 by continuously updating the scheme according to public interest. On approving your scheme, the appropriate commissioner would have set a time period for which the scheme will be valid. It is important to bear in mind any constraints the commissioners may have placed on amending the scheme prior to the end of this time period.

Organisations have an obligation to maintain the scheme as submitted to the respective commissioner for approval, but you may also want to start thinking about scheme development. How frequently will you update your scheme? How will you determine the most effective way to update the scheme, for example, will you add new information to existing classes or will you add new classes to the scheme?

How will you determine the success of your scheme? What information will you need to capture about your requests for information in order to include those of most interest in future amendments to the scheme? Will you place the most commonly requested information in your scheme?

Providing information in an unstructured and illogical manner may frustrate customers and also increase resource implications for your organisation. Information otherwise accessible is exempt under FOI, but if potential applicants are unable to locate information that is in the public domain, the question will simply change from 'can you make information available' to 'where is it'.

The World Wide Web offers an excellent tool through which your organisation can make information available, although any policies on utilising the website should also acknowledge methods of ensuring information is available to all. Obligations under DDA should also be taken into account and website accessibility is a vast subject. You may also have other media through which you are able to make information generally available, and the considerations discussed above will be equally applicable to alternative formats.

Remember, requests under FOI do not have to state why the information is required or for what purpose it will be used. Consequently, it could be assumed that information made available in response to requests is in the public domain and your organisation will cease to have control over who is able to access that information. If your organisation is content making that assumption, using some means, such as your website, to make information generally available will enable you to know what is being placed in the public domain and when.

Your website may also offer an opportunity of reducing resource implications of processing requests for information. For example, rather than producing copies of documents in response to requests, can information more easily be placed on the website? Do you have many requests for similar information? If so, would it be useful to place the most frequent requests onto your website making that information otherwise accessible?

Where does FOI fit into any communications strategy within your organisation and how does that strategy make use of your website? By placing information on your website, would it make enquiries for information easier to deal with at the point of entry to your organisation, if it is feasible for staff to know how to search for information on your website? Would there be other benefits to your organisation by making information available on your website? Should information also be made available on your organisation's intranet? If so, how will links be made between your website and intranet?

This subsection has focused upon utilising your organisation's website, but all the questions are equally applicable to any other means of communications your organisation uses to provide information to the general public.

Summary

Having addressed the issues raised in this chapter, you should now have an understanding and appreciation of:

- activities that need completing in order to process requests received by your organisation;

- who is best placed to complete these activities within your organisation and resource implications;

- the need to track and monitor requests, and the possibility of using existing systems or developing a new supporting application;

- a long-term strategy for placing information held by your organisation into the public domain.

Useful references

General

- Data Protection Act 1998, 1998 Chapter 29, available from HMSO Online: *http://www.legislation.hmso.gov.uk/acts/acts1998/19980029.htm*.

- Statutory Instrument 1992 No. 3240 Environmental Information Regulations 1992 – available from HMSO Online: *http://www.hmso.gov.uk/si/si1992/Uksi_19923240_en_1.htm*.

- Although focused on FOIA, the Department of Constitutional Affairs (DCA) website offers useful advice and guidance on how to deal with requests under FOI that will be useful to organisations across the UK: *http:// www.dca.gov.uk/foi/foidpunit.htm*. For full contact details for the DCA, please see Chapter 2.

FOIA

- Lord Chancellor's Code of Practice on the discharge of public authorities functions under Part I of the Freedom of Information Act 2000. Issued under Section 45 of the Act, November 2002. Available from the Department of Constitutional Affairs (DCA): *http://www.dca.gov.uk/ foi/codepafunc.htm*. For full contact details for the DCA, please see Chapter 2.

- The Information Commissioner's Office (ICO) has made a range of Awareness Guidance available. At the time of this book going to print, there were 13 in the series. The majority deal with exemptions, but there are is also some general guidance available on the public interest test, time for compliance and when information is caught: *http:// www.informationcommissioner.gov.uk/*. For full contact details for the ICO, please see Chapter 2.

FOISA

- Draft Scottish Ministers Code of Practice on the Discharge of Functions by Public Authorities under the Freedom of Information (Scotland) Act 2002. Yet to be laid before the Scottish Parliament. This is available from the Scottish Information Commissioner's (SIC) website: *http://www.itspublicknowledge.info*.

- The monthly newsletter produced by the SIC often offers advice on issues that will affect the provision of information: *http://www.itspublicknowledge.info*. For full contact details for the SIC, please see Chapter 2.

5

Exemptions

Objectives

The objectives of this chapter are to enable you to:

- identify issues that may arise when interpreting and applying exemptions;
- identify where devising policies may be appropriate;
- begin to understand what factors your organisation may need to take into account when considering public interest.

Background

While it is very important that organisations embrace the new culture of openness in order to comply with FOI, there will be instances where there is a genuine need to withhold information from disclosure. A number of exemptions exist under the Acts for this purpose, but in order to be effective, must be consistently applied and understood by those responsible for managing them.

Exemptions also require regular re-evaluation to ensure they remain applicable, which in turn will require adequate audit trails for any decisions taken. Consequently, the management of exemptions and what is thought to be exempt material may be very complex and resource intensive, and therefore requires adequate preparation. Exemptions also provide the interface between FOI and other legislation that may be applicable to information you hold in some circumstances, which is discussed in more detail below.

Specific interpretations of exemptions are not considered in this chapter as there is already some information available (see Useful References at the end of the chapter) and it may be that interpretations change following the implementation of the general right of access.

The focus of this chapter is to examine some of the practical procedures that will need to be implemented to manage exemptions, and how to formulate a consistent approach to balancing public interest against the need to maintain an exemption. It is essential that any procedures remain flexible enough to cope with any changes in interpretation of exemptions and also to react to public interest.

There can be little doubt that some of the content of information that is made accessible under FOI for the first time will be of significant interest to the public and media. However, one element of compliance that will generate public discussion will almost certainly be the use and management of exemptions, especially as many decisions about disclosure may be highly subjective.

Checklist

How will you interpret exemptions?

Under FOI, there are two types of exemptions. The first are those which are termed absolute exemptions. The remaining exemptions are those subject to the public interest test, which under FOIA have become known as qualified exemptions.

In the absence of any case law it may be important for organisation to use an interpretation of the relevant exemptions in order to ensure they can be consistently applied from 1 January 2005. If you have already looked through Chapter 3, you are likely to have an idea about the information your organisation holds that is likely to be of interest, and possibly what information is likely to be exempt from disclosure.

You may also need to decide how to interpret exemptions to ensure consistency with other third-party organisations that hold similar information to your own. There is already some useful guidance available from the UK Information Commissioner's website in the form of fact sheets, with guidance due to be made available by the Office of the Scottish Information Commissioner towards the end of 2004.

Note that if you are intending to use both of these sources for guidance in the management of exemptions, there are different exemptions under the two Acts, and some of the common exemptions are worded differently. Many of the exemptions under FOIA use the term 'prejudice' to determine the harm or implications of disclosing the information. However, FOISA uses the term 'prejudice substantially' which is likely to mean that any harm, threat or implication of disclosing the information will need to be more significant than any assessed under FOIA.

Both Acts are similar in that assessing the need to maintain most of the exemptions, you have to decide whether disclosure 'would, or would be likely to' cause any implications to occur. This means that you cannot withhold information using a hypothetical justification. It is likely that evidence would be needed in order to apply some exemptions, particularly if the applicant complained or requested a review as a result of your organisation withholding information.

If you hold a large volume of information you think may be exempt under FOI, it will be essential to make a plan of how exemptions will be managed. You may need to provisionally decide which exemptions will be applied to various information types, and what justification you have for applying each exemption. However, you should remember that where exemptions are subject to the public interest test, the public interests needs to be balanced against the need to maintain the exemption whenever a request for the information is made. Many of these issues are discussed in further detail below.

What will be your procedure for applying exemptions?

When considering procedures for applying exemptions in your organisation you need to take into account a number of different factors. When will you apply exemptions to material you hold? There are likely to be a number of options for your organisation: you could apply exemptions on creation or receipt (if information is coming into your organisation from a third party) of information, or you could assess exemptions on receiving requests for information.

You may decide that it limits resources to assess the application of exemptions on receipt of requests for inform-ation as the need to maintain many of the exemptions (those subject to the public interest test) will need to be balanced against current public interest at that time. However, using this approach alone could be very time consuming, particularly if you receive a large volume of requests.

The choice of options is likely to depend on the amount of information you hold that is likely to be exempt and also the resources you have do deal with requests for information. For example, is it possible to ask individuals in your organisation to apply exemptions as and when requests are made for information they are responsible for? This is only likely to be feasible if individuals across the organisation hold very different types of information and if your organisation receives a small number of requests for information.

Using this approach for a large number of requests may lead to inconsistencies, and it may be very difficult for you to prove your organisation has taken a consistent approach in the event of any investigations conducted by the commissioner. If exemptions will be applied and justified by those holding the information, how will you ensure staff are applying exemptions appropriately?

Another option may be to initially apply exemptions to certain record types where they can be justified, which will help with consistency. Again, you should not forget that the majority of exemptions will need to be reassessed to take into account the public interest, if the information to which they are applied is requested. If you decide certain record types will be exempt, or that exemptions will be applied to documentation on creation or receipt, you also need to decide how you will review the continued applicability of an exemption.

This may not be required for any absolute exemptions. For example where you hold personal data and placing that information into the public domain would breach the one or more of the Principles of the Data Protection Act, it is highly unlikely that application of the exemption will change with time.

How will you ensure exemptions are consistently applied?

What plans do you need to make for substantially similar information types that exist across your organisation to ensure that they are assessed with consistency? How do you know where these record or information types are in your organisation? Is terminology regarding information and record types used consistently across your organisation? How can you be certain the content of the information is consistent? Are these record or information types used for the same purpose? Different purposes may have caused local changes in the way some information is constructed, particularly in large organisations. This, again, picks up on some of the issues raised in Chapter 3.

What information about exemptions will you record in any monitoring and tracking system?

Will you need to know where information has previously been withheld from disclosure? Would staff need access to previous decisions made about exemptions before disclosing certain information? This may be important where you have information that is a borderline case. Staff who are required to make decisions about disclosure may find it useful to check previous assessments of implications of disclosure, although the public interest may be different each time a request for that information is made.

Another reason for recording information may be to ensure that information withheld by some parts of your organisation is not then subsequently released by another part. There can be little doubt that the disclosure will set a precedent and all departments, perhaps even other organisations, will have to follow the lead.

One final consideration is the information you will need to produce a comprehensive audit trail in the event of your organisation's processing of requests being subject to scrutiny. What factors will you need to document? Will you need to record all information taken into account when deciding whether an exemption should be applied? Decisions to apply exemptions will be relatively simple in some cases, for example, for information otherwise accessible. However, where public interest needs to be taken into account, considerations could become highly complex.

How will you deal with partial disclosures?

There are likely to be many instances where your organisation can make certain elements of information available, but will withhold others. In these circumstances, you may choose to redact the information (controlled removal of the information that you have decided is exempt) or provide the applicant with a summary. In both these scenarios, how will you record what information was actually disclosed to the applicant? How and where will it be filed? How will you make other staff aware of decisions? Again, it is important to note that the exemptions cannot be applied indefinitely and may need to be reassessed when the information is requested again, depending on circumstances.

How familiar with exemptions do staff across your organisation need to be?

This decision will relate to the procedures you use to apply and manage exemptions. You will need methods to identify information that is exempt, procedures to apply the public interest and procedures to deal with disclosure. Depending upon how you choose to apply and manage exemptions will determine the levels of awareness required, although any assessment should also take into account the need to ensure consistency in the use of exemptions.

Do not forget that FOI places obligations on organisations to advice and assist, and therefore all staff may need a basic understanding of FOI. Should this include information about how exemptions are used? In any event, it is likely that a number of queries received by your organisation will relate to the area of exemptions.

Two exemptions relate to requests falling under other legislation (Data Protection Act 1998 and the Environmental Information Regulations), where that legislation places different requirements on your organisation for dealing with requests. Does everyone need to know about these specific exemptions? This specific question is discussed further below, and all of the issues raised above are further addressed in Chapter 7.

How will you evaluate the continued applicability of exemptions?

As discussed in response to a number of questions above, it is likely that when using exemptions subject to the public interest test, the need to maintain that exemption and any associated justification may diminish over the lifecycle of the information. Are you going to proactively review information previously withheld or only reassess exemptions in response to a request? If you are going to proactively review information, how will you make that information accessible if appropriate?

There may also be reasons to review the application of absolute exemptions during the lifecycle of the record or information, or in the event of case law. Where exemptions are reviewed, this should be completed in a controlled and managed manner, taking into consideration issues raised when initially applying the exemption.

This task is unlikely to be a high priority in initial preparations but is worth giving some thought, as other preparations discussed above may help or hinder this task in the future.

Do other organisations have substantially similar information to your organisation?

Where other organisations hold types of information that are substantially similar to the information held by your organisation, it may be worth discussing how you will be using exemptions after 1 January 2005. It could be difficult to successfully argue the use of an exemption for a type of information where another organisation has chosen to disclose it.

Once you have thought about what information you believe may be exempt under FOI, it could be beneficial to share those thoughts with other organisations that hold similar information. Discussions may provide different thoughts on the implications of making information available, which could be useful to your organisation. It may also be that these organisations hold information belonging to your organisation that you believe may be subject to an exemption, which would require discussion. This is discussed in the next question.

What information belonging to your organisation is held by third parties?

This question and the next were posed in Chapter 3 and are developed further here in relation to exemptions. It is essential that under FOI, information is placed in the public domain in a controlled manner. It is likely that there has been a large degree of uncontrolled duplication in most organisations, some of which has been distributed to sources external to your organisation. FOI applies to any information held, therefore you need to make arrangements to protect any information that should be genuinely exempt under FOI which is held by third parties. A different approach may be required for organisations that are subject to FOI and those that are not: the appropriateness of using contracts (taking into account the Section 60 (FOISA) and Section 45 (FOIA) code of practice) to address the issue of information security may be something your organisation needs to consider to ensure the publication of information is as controlled as possible.

How will you make others aware that you have applied exemption to information you may have passed to them? What arrangements do you need to make for the management of information once it is held in a location outside of your organisation? These questions are as equally applicable to information that will not carry an exemption, although this type of information is likely to have fewer implications resulting from disclosure.

What information does your organisation hold that belongs to a third party?

It is likely that your organisation holds a large volume of information that is owned by another organisation, which may be a public or private organisation. Regardless of the source of information, it is likely that it was transferred to your organisation with certain expectations about how that information will be managed in terms of security and accessibility. In many instances, the information may have been transferred prior to FOI and therefore the implications would have been largely unknown.

In these circumstances you need to decide on a number of factors. Should your organisation still be holding that information? Do your records retention and destruction schedules cope with this information? Is the application of exemptions appropriate? To what degree will you consult organisations whose information you hold when you receive a request for that information? Finally you should ensure that you have addressed all considerations you would expect other organisations to address where they are holding your information.

This particular area has the potential to be extremely complex. It may be that the information was given to your organisation under a contract with a confidentiality clause, or in circumstances where disclosure would cause a breach of confidence actionable by the person to whom the information belongs. In these circumstances, the information may be protected by an absolute exemption, but it is likely in the majority of situations there will no signed agreements or record of decisions made at the time.

The area of confidentiality is extremely complex and you may wish to take legal advice in some cases before making decisions about disclosure.

How will your organisation assess public interest for each request?

There is already some guidance available in this area in codes of practice under both Acts. Under FOIA, organisations are able to extend the 20 working-day time limit for processing requests 'until such time as is reasonable in the circumstances' in order to make a decision, but there is no such allowance under FOISA. This type of decision has the potential to be highly subjective, and therefore you should try to make assessments in the most consistent manner possible, and ensure you keep adequate records. Failure to attempt to achieve consistency in considering public interest will almost certainly lead to complaints against your organisation.

When information is requested that is subject to a public interest exemption, on a very simplistic level, you need to assess public interest and then harm in disclosing and balance the two. Who will assess public interest and authorise the application (or continued application) of an exemption from disclosure? Do you need a group who make decisions in a centralised manner, or will you ask individuals to make decisions about exemptions?

How will you decide what the effect and implications of disclosing the information will be, particularly in the early stages of 2005? At what point will you consult any third parties that may have an interest in the information, if you are going to consult them? What information do you need to record about assessing the public interest at any given time?

You should also remember the requirements stated the relevant codes of practice when communicating the withholding of information due to an exemption subject to the public interest test. Under both Acts, you are required to state the reasons you believe the public interest in maintaining the exemption outweighs the public interest in disclosure. You also need to specify the factors you have used taken into account both for and against disclosure, with the code of practice under FOISA placing a duty on organisations to explain those factors to applicants.

How will you determine whether disclosure will result in 'prejudice' (under FOIA) or 'substantial prejudice' (under FOISA)?

This is likely to be a highly subjective area, that is almost entirely dependent on the particular set of information being considered. It may be that it can be demonstrated that the disclosure of certain record types will have specific implications, but this is likely to be exceptional. As previously stated, the implications from disclosing the information must be 'real', and therefore you cannot take into account any hypothetical outcomes.

One approach may be to list implications which are known to have resulted from putting certain information into the public domain. These can then be used as a set of criteria against which future requests can be assessed. This list is likely to increase after 1 January 2005, and it will be extremely important to monitor decisions taken by other organisations and any impact resulting from those decisions.

How will you document your policies regarding the management of exemptions?

The management of exemptions is likely to be of significant interest once FOI is fully enforced. If you decide on policies for managing exemptions, it may be useful for you to make that information accessible, helping you to respond to enquiries about exemptions and also provide information and guidance to staff.

It is very important that these policies can be integrated into other policies in your organisation, particularly those regarding information and records. However, you may also need to give some thought to what other documentation will be required in order to implement the policy. The management of exemptions may be extremely complex and therefore you may also need complementary guidance and procedures for staff to follow in a range of circumstances.

How will you manage the interface between FOI, data protection and EIRs?

Two of the exemptions under FOI provide an interface with other legislation, namely the Data Protection Act 1988 (DPA) for personal data, and the Environmental Information Regulations (EIRs) for any environmental information held by your organisation. If your organisation holds either personal data or environmental information, it is important that you are aware of where this information is held, and what procedures are in place to make certain that requests are not inappropriately handled.

As a starting point, how will you ensure requests are processed under the appropriate legislation? It will be extremely important to ensure that all staff in your organisation are familiar with the high-level differences between FOI and DPA if you hold personal data in your organisation. It is important to note that FOI does not have a 'blanket' exemption for personal data, but for personal data where disclosure would breach one of the data protection principles. Consequently, there may be information previously deemed personal data and therefore thought to be protected under DPA, which will be disclosable under FOI.

Guidance issued by the UK Commissioner has already indicated that at least some information relating to an individual in the professional capacity within the public sector will be disclosable. It is therefore important for your organisation to make decisions about what information about staff it is reasonable to disclose under FOI. Information such as personal appraisals will clearly remain subject to the provisions of DPA, but the boundary is not so clear cut for a number of other areas relating to an individual's role. Again, it may be important to take appropriate legal advice in some circumstances.

A request for information does have an absolute exemption where an applicant is requesting personal data about him or herself. This should be processed as a Subject Access Request, which has different time limits and restrictions on how the request should be processed.

The EIRs also have slightly different requirements from FOI, with the most important being that requests for environmental information can be made verbally. You therefore need to ensure that you have the necessary procedures in place to ensure your organisation does not inadvertently breach other legislation governing information in an effort to comply with FOI. Environmental Information Regulations also have exceptions rather than exemptions, which, once you have investigated the EIRs' requirements, you may choose to manage in the same way as FOI exemptions.

Summary

Having addressed the issues raised in this chapter, you should now have an understanding and appreciation of:

- how exemptions will need to be managed within your organisation;

- what documentation, in terms of policies and procedures, you will need in order to ensure consistency;

- the boundaries between FOI and other legislation that may govern the information you hold including DPA 1998 and the EIRs.

Useful references

- Relatively little information is currently available regarding exemptions. Information is starting to appear on public authority websites with regard to policies, which you should find through searching the Internet.

- The Constitution Unit at UCL offers a range of publications on FOI, including some on exemptions. A list of these can be found at *http://www.ucl.ac.uk/ constitutionunit/foidp/publications.php* and their telephone number is 020 7679 4977.

FOIA

- The Information Commissioner's Office (ICO) has made a range of Awareness Guidance available. At the time of this book going to print, there were 13 in the series. Those on exemptions include:

  □ Personal Information

  □ Information Provided in Confidence

  □ The Public Interest Test

  □ Legal Professional Privilege Section 42

  □ Commercial Interest, together with an annex on public sector contracts

□ Information Reasonably Accessible to the Applicant by Other Means

□ Information Intended for Future Publication

□ Information Contained in Court Records

□ Defence Exemption

□ Relations within the UK.

The above can be found on the website: *http:// informationcommissioner.gov.uk*. For full contact details for the ICO, please see Chapter 2.

FOISA

■ The Scottish Information Commissioner is aiming to publish briefings during the second half of 2004. Their website is *http://itspublicknowledge.info/*.

6

Audit trails, proving compliance and other considerations

Objectives

The objectives of this chapter are to enable you to:

- identify the requirements for monitoring how requests are dealt with;
- decide what audit trails your organisation will need to prove compliance with FOI;
- examine the necessary procedures for handling complaints or reviews.

Background

In order to prove compliance, organisations will need as a minimum a record that demonstrates what actions they took and why they were taken. Under codes of practice associated with both Acts, there are requirements to capture certain statistics with some of the specific text already discussed in Chapter 4. These requirements are examined further in the checklist below.

The way in which audit trails are approached will depend on the size and function of organisation, procedures established to deal with requests and to some extent, the number of requests. Any system that is implemented must take into account requirements to capture data associated with requests and the potential resource implications of this task. There may also be benefits to your organisation in capturing data about requests. Monitoring and reporting trends, particularly if your organisation tends to have a high media profile, may be useful and requirements should be built into any system designed to capture information from the outset.

It should be noted that this is one area where the Acts are different in terms of what they specify has to be captured and what course of action an applicant should take if they are in any way dissatisfied with the outcome of their request. Consequently the checklist is brief, but this area should be examined in more detail by your organisation to ensure you have adequate measures in place to ensure compliance.

This topic, more so than many of the other elements of FOI, will depend upon many factors that could be substantially different across organisations. This chapter is intentionally short, focusing on high level considerations that need to be developed and taken forward.

Checklist

How will you collate and report statistics?

One of the first considerations should be the requirements of reporting statistics associated with the Acts. The code of practice associated with Section 45 of FOIA states:

For monitoring purposes public authorities should keep a record of all applications where either all or part of the requested information is withheld. In addition to a record of the numbers of applications involved where the information is withheld, senior managers in each public authority need information on each case to determine whether cases are properly considered, and whether the reasons for refusal are sound.

This requirement raises a number of issues. How will you capture the numbers of requests where information is either entirely or partly withheld? What information do you need to record about a case in order to prove a request has been 'properly considered, and the reasons for refusal were sound'? Which senior management role will evaluate a case to determine whether the initial request was adequately dealt with?

Given the code of practice is not specific as to what information about a request should be held, your organisation may need to evaluate information held about cases and requests, analysing any lessons learnt and changing processes as necessary. It may also be useful to consult with other organisations once FOI has been implemented, with a view to establishing the most appropriate practice for dealing with requests. However, in order to prepare for 1 January 2005, it is important to decide on a procedure for evaluating the processing of requests and be prepared to amend that procedure if it is not fit for purpose.

The code of practice under FOIA also specifies records relating to complaints should be kept together with the outcome of that complaint.

FOISA is different in that the draft code of practice associated with Section 60 has a specific section on the monitoring of requests. Under this section, the code places a specific obligation on authorities to monitor their own performance under FOI. The following are suggested as statistics which may be indicative of performance:

- the number of requests for information that have been refused and the reasons for refusal;

- fees which have been charged;

- reviews (see below) that have been carried out and the outcome of those reviews;

- instances when the time limit for reply has been exceeded and the reasons why it has been exceeded.

While recording elements of performance will help your organisation continually monitor and report on compliance with FOI, it is essential that the capture of the statistics does not result in yet more work. Often, when devising performance indicators, it is relatively easy to think of a statistic that will demonstrate performance, however, you also need to give thought to the calculation. Can the information actually be captured? Will you need to filter out any additional information? If so, how will this be done and how long will it take?

Does the statistic need to take into account any other factors? If so, how will they be included and accounted for? Can the statistic chosen also be affected by any factors that are not within the control of your organisation? If so, it may not be the best statistic to choose as a representation of your performance. Will the statistic be accurate? If you are choosing not to record every request, it is possible that any statistics you report may be inaccurate. See the next question below for further considerations.

With a little extra thought at the outset, collecting and reporting statistics may also help keep track of the resources required for your organisation to comply with FOI.

This type of information will be useful to you and senior management when making any long term strategies for dealing with FOI and information management.

How will you prove compliance for individual requests?

Although you may be able to capture information that shows a good performance under FOI, you also need to decide how you will prove compliance for an individual request. It is highly likely that in many organisations some requests will not be recorded at all, where, for example, the information is otherwise accessible. Staff are likely to be able to quickly and efficiently deal with this request and there will be little organisational benefit to justify the time required to capture information about this request.

Consequently it is feasible that an applicant could be dissatisfied with a request of which you have no record in your organisation. It should be unlikely, but it is an issue you need to factor into how you process requests, which was discussed in Chapter 4.

Similarly, taking the example provided by FOISA of recording requests that exceed their time limit. You may choose to measure this as an indication of performance under FOI but there may be instances where the request is initially assessed and the complexity not understood. A simple request could simply be mismanaged causing the request to go over the time limit. If you are choosing not to record every request, both of these cases have the potential to go unrecorded. Therefore there will be no audit trail of actions taken, which may appear inconsistent from an applicant's perspective, and the request will not be included in any statistics produced.

As with the majority of questions in this book, there are no right or wrong answers when making your preparations. What is important is that you decide a way forward for your organisation, but make adequate plans to evaluate activities and change the way in which you deal with FOI, responding to issues when they arise as appropriate.

What action will your organisation take if an applicant is dissatisfied with the handling of a request for information?

In the Section 45 Code of Practice associated with FOIA, it states that any expression of dissatisfaction with regard to the way in which a legitimate request for information under FOI has been handled should be treated as a complaint. While FOISA does not have the same wording in the respective code, it also suggests that dissatisfaction should trigger the 'review' process, which is a specific process detailed by FOISA, discussed below.

Under FOIA, an applicant is entitled to make a complaint to the organisation if they are dissatisfied with the way in which a request has been handled. Organisations are obliged under the Act to communicate to the applicant their rights of complaint. Organisations should also inform the applicant how to make a complaint should they wish to do so. FOIA entitles an applicant to complain directly to the UK Information Commissioner where an authority has failed to set up an adequate complaints procedure.

FOISA specifies a more detailed process for dissatisfied applicant, which it terms a 'requirement for review'. The code of practice (Section 60) distinguishes this requirement from an organisations existing complaints procedure. The code also suggests that where the complaint concerns a request for information under the general right of access, the review should be carried out by staff who did not handle the original request. Unlike FOIA where authorities can set their own target times, FOISA states that requirements for reviews must be dealt within 20 working days.

How will you define a 'complaint'? What will the process be for dealing with that issue? What information do you need to record about a complaint or requirement for review? How will you decide which staff should be involved in complaints processes? How will those staff access each case and what information from the original request will they need to make a fair assessment? What provisions will you make for cases where information about the original case is not available?

Under both Acts, where the original decision of the authority is upheld, the right of appeal to the appropriate commissioner must be included in any response to the applicant.

What information will your organisation need to deal with a request investigated by the commissioner?

Should an applicant complain to the commissioner, you will need records to show how your organisation acted in response to the initial request and why, and subsequent communications and justification for each of those actions. What information is required to justify actions taken? How will you consistently record it? Will you hold information about requests centrally or will you collate the information? If so, how long will it take to collate? This will be particularly important where the public interest has been taken into account when taking decisions about disclosure of information. It is quite possible the public interest in certain information will be different by the time any request is reviewed by the commissioner and your records will therefore be vital in proving compliance.

If your organisation is likely to receive a small number of requests, holds no information that is contentious or sensitive, and does not generally have a high public profile, you may never need to undertake this task. However, you should still be aware of potential outcomes and factor this element of compliance into preparations. While every organisation would hope they will never be in a position where they need to justify actions taken to the commissioner, it is inevitable that dissatisfaction will be escalated to that level for some organisations. Providing you have been adequately prepared, you should have all the necessary measures in place to justify how the request has been handled and prove compliance with FOI.

Summary

Having addressed the issues raised in this chapter, you should now have an understanding and appreciation of:

- how to demonstrate your organisation's performance under FOI and how you will prove compliance;
- how to recognise a complaint under FOIA and the need for a requirement for review under FOISA;
- the procedures necessary for dealing with complaints or reviews with ideas about who will conduct those procedures, and the information and records that will be involved and generated.

Useful references

FOIA

- Lord Chancellor's Code of Practice on the discharge of public authorities functions under Part I of the Freedom of Information Act 2000. Issued under Section 45 of the Act, November 2002. Available from the Department of Constitutional Affairs (DCA): *http://www.dca.gov.uk/foi/ codepafunc.htm*. For full contact details for the DCA, please see Chapter 2.

FOISA

- Draft Scottish Ministers Code of Practice on the Discharge of Functions by Public Authorities under the Freedom of Information (Scotland) Act 2002. Yet to be laid before the Scottish Parliament. This is available from the Scottish Information Commissioner's (SIC) website: *http://www.itspublicknowledge.info*. For full contact details for the SIC, please see Chapter 2.

7

Training

Objectives

The objectives of this chapter are to enable you to:

- identify high-level training activities that may be appropriate for your organisation;
- identify tasks, groups or individuals that may require specialist training;
- examine some of the constraints there may be when implementing a training programme in your organisation.

Background

Having made a plan of preparations for the arrival of FOI, it is important to communicate the implications to staff across your organisation and ensure all staff know what is expected of them in order to comply with legislation. It is likely that all staff will either hold, create, or make use of information in order to fulfil their role, therefore FOI can potentially have an impact on them.

Training is also necessary to ensure requests are dealt with in accordance with the legislation. Requests for information can be made to anyone in the organisation and do not have to mention the Act. As soon as the request is received, the 20 working-day clock starts ticking. If applicants are unsure of the exact information they are looking for, there is also a duty to advise and assist. Even if you are to try and coordinate this role in a central function, it will still be important that all staff are aware of this arrangement, and how to process the initial enquiry.

A training programme may take a number of different forms depending on the learning needs of staff, state of readiness of organisation and the way in which you have chosen to process requests for information. Any programme should not forget the important cultural issues as well as management of information and records, which will be an important ingredient of successful compliance.

You also need to give some thought when constructing the initial training programme about how an ongoing training programme will be designed in order to take into account new staff and any case law that affects the way in which you deal with FOI.

As with Chapter 3, which looked at managing information and records, the area of training must have careful consideration with proper training needs analysis in order to be successful. This chapter should provide you with an overview of necessary tasks for compliance with FOI, who will complete those tasks and what their training needs might be. This then needs to be developed with the appropriate staff in your organisation. Some options for training and awareness raising are also discussed in the checklist below.

Checklist

What is the current level of awareness of FOI and its implications in your organisation?

A good starting point when thinking about training in any subject is to make a high-level assessment of awareness across the organisation, which will contribute to decisions regarding the most appropriate means of training. Ideally, as you have been making other preparations for FOI, you will have been consulting others across the organisation and using their input to formulate solutions for issues that arise. Consequently some groups or individuals may have a fairly good understanding of FOI and the potential impact on your organisation.

In order to move forward, you need to decide how you will assess 'awareness'. What knowledge of the Act do your staff need to have? How will they need to use this knowledge and under what circumstances? This will depend upon the way you have decided to process requests and manage associated tasks, such as the application of exemptions. How will you decide what level of understanding your staff need to have? What are the risks with staff being inadequately trained?

What roles in your organisation will deal with the implications of FOI and what is the most appropriate means of training for each role?

Starting with all staff, there is a duty to advise and assist all potential applicants under FOI. It is therefore likely that all staff will need a basic awareness of FOI in order to comply with this obligation. What is the most effective message of communicating information to all staff? Do you have forums or media that are already used effectively to inform staff of important information that could be used for FOI? Have there been any previous training programmes that would provide information about the most effective way to train all staff? Implementing a training programme can be very time consuming and costly and it will be very important that you choose a method that is appropriate for your organisation and staff, and for the task in hand.

Have you identified 'FOI champions'? What training, if any, will they require? What other roles have you identified as being necessary in order to comply having completed the previous chapters? For example, who will be managing exemptions? Who will be managing the requests received by your organisation? This may be individuals or groups. What training will they need? It is likely that some groups or individuals will require specialist training in order to complete their tasks, and training may need to be prioritised to ensure that those that are a high priority can be trained within time and cost constraints.

In addition, look beyond 1 January 2005. Which tasks will need to become routine in order to continue complying with FOI? How will you make information available that is contained in your publication scheme? Is there any information in your scheme that has not previously been made available and may contain exemptions? If so, you need to decide processes for removing information you believe to be exempt, how to store the revised information, and how you indicate in the information concerned that some has been removed. All of these activities may require staff to be trained, particularly to ensure consistency in approach across your organisation, that your organisation fulfils its legal obligations and you are able to manage information effectively.

Various chapters have discussed relationships with third parties. Where you identified that these third parties need to be involved in FOI preparations, their training needs should also be considered. How will you raise awareness with third parties that your organisation works or deals with on a regular basis? Remember that the Acts refer to information held and not owned and therefore if you are holding third-party information, the third party may be affected by FOI.

What are the staff learning requirements and what interventions could meet these requirements?

Once you have identified all the groups of people that require training, you need to spend some time looking at specific learning requirements. This may include some kind of gap analysis, evaluation of how people will need to apply their new skills, a thorough training or learning needs analysis and developing an overview of how each of the roles you have identified will interact.

This task may be extremely complex and it is likely to be worth consulting with any learning or development function you have in your organisation for ideas about how various issues can be taken forward. Again, it is important to factor in how you will ensure continued compliance. Which roles need to remain flexible in their approach to FOI due to unknown implications? How much could an individual's role change once FOI comes into force as a result of experience gained by your organisation or case law? When staff who have a specialist FOI role leave, how will you decide who will take up their role? How will you train new staff who are assigned specialist roles?

Another important consideration is the impact of FOI on core business processes. Some staff may not be directly involved in preparing for FOI, but where the legislation may impact on business processes, staff may require training in order to change the way they complete existing tasks.

How much time and money is available for training staff?

This is an extremely important question, as the response may significantly affect the options available to you. It is important to establish any budget for training staff in preparation for FOI, in addition to any ongoing budgetary requirements for routine training.

You may also need to look at other staff commitments around the time you are intending to conduct FOI training. The effectiveness of training could be substantially reduced if you choose a time when staff are already undertaking other training initiatives or it is the busiest time of the year for staff in their roles.

One option may be to integrate FOI into other training that is already planned. This method is unlikely to have such a high impact, but could offer the advantage of highlighting how FOI has the potential to impact all areas of the business. You should, however, look to incorporate FOI into existing training where appropriate, for example, any information management (IM) or records management (RM) training or any training that deals with managing customers of your organisation.

What are the risks of not training staff?

Given the proximity to 1 January 2005, there could be obstacles preventing completion of a training programme before that time. Therefore you should spend some time assessing the risks that may manifest should staff in your organisation not be trained.

To what extent will you train staff about exemptions?

Certain aspects of FOI are likely to attract the most interest and the management of exemptions will be one of those areas for many organisations, particularly those that hold sensitive or contentious information that they may deem exempt. Therefore, in deciding how to manage exemptions, you need to decide exactly what staff need to know about exemptions in order to adequately manage them.

It may be that your organisation holds very little information that is likely to be exempt and therefore staff do not have any requirement to understand exemptions. However, if you are likely to expect staff to be using exemptions regularly, you may need to provide staff with training. This will be particularly important where staff share information with third parties, and you have identified a need to communicate your organisation's view on exemptions covering the material prior to passing it to another organisation subject to FOI. It is also important to ensure staff understand the need for controlled and managed disclosure of information, and that staff do not think that FOI authorises them to personally disclose information, unless this forms part of the procedures you have devised.

This question has specifically addressed exemptions, but there may be other elements of FOI that will be particularly relevant to your organisation. From work covered in previous chapters, you should have taken some steps towards identifying these areas. You need to ask similar questions to those above to ascertain whether you need specific training to deal with these areas of FOI. These may include procedures for managing requests to conclusion where you have decided to fully distribute procedures for managing requests. Another area that may be relevant to your organisation is training that enables staff to distinguish between the different legislation governing information you hold. This will again depend on the procedures you have decided to use and also the type of information that is held by your organisation.

How will you build FOI into induction programmes?

This may not be a priority consideration, but it is important that the area is dealt with at some point in your preparations. It is vital to ensure that all new staff understand the fundamental concepts of FOI and what their obligations are as a member of staff in your organisation.

You will have already decided the minimum level of knowledge that each member of staff should have if you have answered the questions above. It may be that this will be appropriate to use as part of an induction for any new staff joining your organisation. However, do not forget about the other elements of compliance with FOI, such as IM and RM. It may be that you need a different approach for those who do not have a developed business knowledge or who are not familiar with the way in which your organisation manages information.

It is also important to remember that your obligations under the Acts could be interpreted in different ways as case law becomes available. Therefore, some kind of communication mechanism to transfer messages and updates to all staff may prove invaluable. Should you decide on a method, the way in which staff should access this information could be incorporated into any training to ensure staff become familiar with the way in which information will be communicated.

How will you deliver training?

Having responded to the questions above, you now need to take forward practical delivery. This checklist should have provided you with sufficient information to start work on this with those in your organisation who specialise in learning, training or staff development.

Summary

Having addressed the issues raised in this chapter, you should now have an understanding and appreciation of:

- the different roles across your organisation required for compliance with FOI and have started to identify their training needs;
- factors that will influence the construction and implementation of any training programme;
- training requirements beyond 1 January 2005.

Useful references

FOIA

- The Department of Constitutional Affairs (DCA) has a Training and Awareness section within the FOI area under Implementing the Act: *http://www.dca.gov.uk/foi/foidpunit.htm*. For full contact details for the DCA, please see Chapter 2.

FOISA

■ The Scottish Executive has a section within the FOI area of their website dedicated to training and has produced a suite of materials for use by authorities that are to comply with FOISA, which is very comprehensive. These materials are listed as publications at: *http://www.scotland.gov.uk/Topics/Government/FOI*. For full contact details for the Scottish Executive, please see Chapter 2.

8

Evaluating success and organisational benefits

Objectives

The objectives of this chapter are to enable you to:

- identify how to measure the success of your FOI preparations;
- quantify benefits to the organisation where possible;
- begin to formulate a strategy for dealing with FOI in the long term.

Background

As with any project or set of preparations, it is essential to identify at what point they become complete and how successful the preparations have been in identifying critical issues. This is not an easy task for FOI preparations as, for many reasons, 'success' is difficult to define at this point in time. Furthermore, in the absence of any case law prior to the implementation of FOI, the point at which you deem your organisation 'ready' can become a moving target.

What is important is that your organisation determines what factors will represent success, and that there is adequate flexibility in the approach to FOI to cater for any unforeseen requirements. Once compliance can be routinely demonstrated, there is a further opportunity to assess other benefits of the FOI preparation programme to the organisation.

Equally there will be a need to determine the appropriate strategic approach to long-term tasks to ensure continued compliance. Again, it is vital that any strategy prioritises core business processes and associated information management (IM), integrating the emerging FOI requirements. It is imperative that FOI preparations, both now and in the long term, take into account the strategic view of IM to ensure there is not divergence between the IM and records management (RM) needs of the organisation and plans for compliance with FOI.

This is the final chapter and is again fairly short, as this area relies heavily upon the preparations you have prioritised for your organisation and what you envisage the impact of FOI to be. This will be substantially different across a range of organisations and therefore the checklist below provides very high-level considerations which you can then develop as appropriate for your organisation.

Checklist

What are your indicators of success going to be in terms of preparations for FOI?

Compliance with the legislation is perhaps the most obvious answer but, as stressed throughout the book, it should not be the only consideration. There are a number of areas that you could look to for indicators: risks that you have identified and indicators showing successful management;

you could use the statistics generated to prove compliance discussed in previous chapters; you may also choose indicators linked to existing core business processes to show a more general improvement in IM or perhaps even customer enquiries.

Can you immediately identify any tangible organisational benefits by making your information more accessible?

There may be current issues existing in your organisation that can be addressed or resolved by the better sharing of information, and it is this type of issue that can be used to positively market FOI. However, you will need to look carefully at why the issue identified is currently viewed as problematic. There may be information security issues, or technical reasons why the information is not shared. It will be very important not to raise expectations beyond a level you are able to meet. It is also important to examine existing issues to ensure they will not result in non-compliance.

Are there any information flows either to or from your organisation that could be improved by allowing greater access to the information? Are there information systems that allow the sharing of information that are currently under-utilised? Is there an opportunity to review issues regarding the volume of information your organisation has to deal with, and find alternative ways of providing access to information that are also FOI compliant? Are there opportunities to rationalise business processes or combine information sources used by staff across your organisation?

There are likely to be a large number of avenues to explore in response to this question, and a simple analysis is likely to be worthwhile in many cases. In addition to positively marketing FOI, it may also help achieve staff 'buy in' to the project, allowing a more comprehensive involvement from your organisation in FOI preparations.

How could your organisation benefit from better IM?

Leading on from the above, this is a far broader issue. It also has the potential to be a very complex question, and could also be highly subjective. However, if you have completed the checklist in Chapter 3, you should have started to understand how better IM could improve the effectiveness or efficiency of core business processes. Ideally, this question should be fully considered to ensure that FOI preparations are not divergent with IM and RM in your organisation, however time and cost are likely to be major factors in an organisation's ability to complete this task.

Does your organisation already have an IM or RM strategy? If so, it will be extremely important to integrate FOI preparations with these strategies. Existing strategies may also highlight organisational objectives that FOI can help to achieve. If there are strategies in place, it is possible that they have not recognised the necessary culture change to a more open and transparent way of working and changes may need to be made to the strategy.

If your organisation has not traditionally recognised IM, now may be the time to start. There can be little doubt that there will be greater scrutiny of how organisations conduct business once FOI comes into force, and it is important that your organisation accurately represents business undertaken in the information it is generating. Again, as stressed throughout, it is important that FOI preparations take into account information needs of the business. This is likely to be very difficult where IM is not formally recognised or there is no overall responsibility for information in your organisation.

What are your strategic goals in terms of FOI and information management?

It may be that you have already decided on what your strategic goals should be and these have helped you shape your programme of preparations. However, if FOI and the management of information and records is a new concept for your organisation, you should set your strategic goals to ensure your preparations remain focused and have direction. Without setting strategic goals that address overall IM needs, it is possible that your preparations will be the perceived minimum for compliance with FOI. While this approach may work for some organisations, what if your assessment of the minimum requirements is inaccurate? Processing requests could become extremely resource intensive and your organisation may suffer from adverse publicity.

What are your organisation's goals and objectives? Can the principles of FOI or more effective IM help achieve these? What would be the effect of non-compliance on these goals and objectives? Will there be a need to reassess the goals you have set? If so, when would be an appropriate time to conduct this assessment?

This question could be fundamental to your preparations, but will be heavily dependent upon the current situation in your organisation. Once you have started reviewing the status of your organisation in terms of readiness for FOI, it would be useful at that time to identify exactly what your objectives are.

How will you evaluate appropriateness of preparations and record lessons learnt?

Given the potential impact on some organisations, it will be vital that preparations made for FOI are fully evaluated and any lessons learnt are recorded for use both in dealing with FOI in the long term and for future projects. It is important not to forget at any point in your preparations that the need to comply with FOI will continue after 1 January 2005 and the activities required from an organisation may change.

It will be extremely important to review whether or not your preparations are adequate at various intervals once FOI comes into force, although the timings are likely to depend upon the number of requests you receive and the outcomes of any complaints procedures. It may also be that some of your preparations were not appropriate for the true implications that are realised after 1 January 2005.

When you are planning your preparations, it may be useful to decide when you will review the effectiveness of the procedures in place. Will these reviews be time-based or if certain activities take place? You may also choose to use trigger points, for example, once you receive a certain number of requests. It is likely that there will be significant interest in FOI at the beginning of 2005, and therefore you should ensure you are not attempting to alter processes that you have devised unless absolutely essential during this period.

How will you decide whether preparations have been appropriate? What activities will you evaluate and why? What information will you need to evaluate the activities you have chosen? How will you obtain feedback from staff and factor it into changes made? How will you use any success factors identified? Will you use performance information to initiate changes?

How will you record lessons learnt? Does your organisation have an existing procedure in place to conduct this task? Can these lessons help you improve the efficiency or effectiveness with which you are dealing with FOI?

After making all your preparations, what risks are you left with managing?

Risk has been a key consideration throughout the book, but there will be risks that you are left with managing on completion of your preparations. Indeed, your preparations may present new risks that to your organisation.

Does your organisation have a central risk register or method of managing risk? How are you going to record and manage risks associated with FOI? Who will evaluate the priority of the risk to your organisation and means of dealing with the issues identified? Does the area of risk need a separate method of communication from the FOI preparations and if so, who needs to be kept informed?

The area of risk can be highly complex and is dealt with by a wide range of sources, some of which are in the Useful References section. However, once again, it is likely to be beneficial to determine how risk is currently managed by your organisation, and also how successfully it is managed. This should provide you with some indication of the most appropriate way to manage risk resulting from FOI.

When will you decide on a long-term strategy for dealing with FOI?

Having made preparations for 1 January 2005, it is important to decide the long-term strategy your organisation should implement to continue compliance with FOI and also respond as necessary to issues that may arise. One of the reasons it would be useful to consider this issue at the outset is that you are likely to need to quantify implications of FOI on your organisation when proposing a strategy. As with the formulation of any strategy, there is a wide range of considerations that will be determined by the nature of your organisation. From an FOI perspective, some of the issues are addressed by the questions below.

Will you be able to use statistics generated by monitoring and tracking procedures in order accurately examine resource implications? Would minor adjustments to statistics you have decided to capture enable you to quantify the amount of time your organisation is spending managing FOI? Will you be able to use a supporting system to start identifying trends in the volume of requests and the type of information requested? Are there any future plans to integrate FOI with another area of the business?

How will performance reporting relate to a strategy? Would targets be useful for future compliance? If so, will you have sufficient data to set realistic targets that would be meaningful? Does a strategy for dealing with FOI need to incorporate other strategic aims such as those for information and knowledge management? When is the most appropriate time, in terms of FOI, for your organisation to set a long-term strategy?

Summary

Having addressed the issues raised in this chapter, you should now have an understanding and appreciation of:

- which factors will demonstrate the success of your preparations;

- the need for continued compliance with FOI;
- the risk that you are left with managing on completion of your plan for preparations.

Useful references

General

- Many of the references provided in Chapter 3 will give you some ideas about the benefits improved IM could bring to your organisation. You will need to look through the information provided and decide what is appropriate for your organisation. One of the best for providing targets and possible success factors would be the appropriate model action plan for achieving compliance.

- The area of risk is vast and it may be that you already have someone in your organisation that is responsible for managing risk. However, one option is to use the Management of Risk section in the OGC PRINCE 2 manual (Office of Government Commerce (2002) Managing Successful Projects with PRINCE 2, third edition, London, The Stationery Office).

FOIA

- Lord Chancellor's code of practice on the discharge of public authorities functions under Part I of the Freedom of Information Act 2000. Issued under Section 45 of the Act, November 2002. Available from the DCA website: *http://www.dca.gov.uk/foi/codepafunc.htm.*

FOISA

- Draft Scottish Ministers code of practice on the Discharge
  of Functions by Public Authorities under the Freedom
  of Information (Scotland) Act 2002. Yet to be laid before
  the Scottish Parliament. This is available from the
  Scottish Information Commissioner's website: *http://www
  .itspublicknowledge.info.*